Reviews of this book

"*Know Your Value* provides a valuable insight to our potential, but most importantly how to capitalise on our hard earned knowledge."

Paul Steggall, Director, e business people (an e business search consultancy)

"The central theme of the book . . . is unique in the knowledge management literature. Much of what has been written in the field focuses on the larger organization/corporate unit of analysis for knowledge management. This book focuses on the individual/personal unit of analysis."

Chuck Seeley, Director, Knowledge Management, Warner-Lambert Company

"Just like organizations, every person needs to be their own knowledge manager. This is a fascinating exploration of understanding and managing the dimension intrinsic to effectiveness."

Andrew Mayo, Director, MLI Ltd

". . . a significant text that needs to be built into all serious management and personal development programme processes. I believe that this book has the potential to reconfigure our personal software to refocus on essential behaviour and processes for survival in the e-enabled K economy."

Victor Newman, Director, Knowledge Development Centre, Cranfield University

"The book provides a new and important perspective of a much written about subject and leads the way to developing personal knowledge in a way that is missed by more traditional approaches to organizational learning."

Edward Truch, Director, Henley Knowledge Management Forum

". . . a refreshing new focus on individual capability and how we might optimize our personal, sometimes vast knowledge resources. I suspect that the application of his [the author's] ideas will speed up the inevitable transition to new forms of relationship between individuals, companies and markets."

Dr Kenneth Stott, Associate Dean, Nangang Technological University, Singapore

"Could be the essential self-help guide for the knowledge age, when more than ever before, our personal marketability is knowledge-based."

Geoff Smith, Business Development Manager, Knowledge Transformation Services, Cap Gemini UK

"I have been inspired by the book to be far more rigorous in deciding what knowledge I need to acquire, how I will achieve this, and then to deliver on the promise to myself. Mick has made a significant contribution to the development of knowledge management thinking by turning it into a construct which each and every individual can use."

Marc Baker, Director Knowledge Management, Post Office Consulting

"Required reading for anyone wanting to attain their true value in the new economy and an important new tool for the organizational KM practitioner."

Owen L.F. Wilson, Principal Consultant, Knowledge Management, CMG Telecom & eBusiness Division

Know your value?

FINANCIAL TIMES
Prentice Hall

In an increasingly competitive world, it is quality
of thinking that gives an edge – an idea that opens new
doors, a technique that solves a problem, or an insight
that simply helps make sense of it all.

We work with leading authors in the fields of
management and finance to bring cutting-edge thinking and
best learning practice to a global market.

Under a range of leading imprints, including
Financial Times Prentice Hall, we create world-class
print publications and electronic products giving readers
knowledge and understanding which can then be
applied, whether studying or at work.

To find out more about our business and professional
products, you can visit us at www.business-minds.com

For other Pearson Education publications, visit
www.pearsoned-ema.com

Pearson
Education

Know your value?

Manage your knowledge and make it pay

Mick Cope

FINANCIAL TIMES
Prentice Hall

An imprint of Pearson Education

London • New York • San Francisco • Toronto • Sydney • Tokyo • Singapore
Hong Kong • Cape Town • Madrid • Amsterdam • Munich • Paris • Milan

PEARSON EDUCATION LIMITED

Head Office
Edinburgh Gate
Harlow CM20 2JE
Tel: +44 (0)1279 623623
Fax: +44 (0)1279 431059

London Office:
128 Long Acre, London WC2E 9AN
Tel: +44 (0)20 7447 2000
Fax: +44 (0)20 7240 5771
Website: www.business-minds.com

....

First published in Great Britain in 2000

ISBN 0 273 65032 7

British Library Cataloguing in Publication Data
A CIP catalogue record for this book can be obtained from the British Library.

10 9 8 7 6 5 4 3 2 1

Typeset by M Rules
Printed and bound in Great Britain by Biddles Ltd, Guildford & King's Lynn

The Publishers' policy is to use paper manufactured from sustainable forests.

For Carmel McConnell
– a rich wellspring of ideas and passion;
and Dave Chitty
– for giving me space to rant.

About the author

Mick Cope is an experienced and inspirational consultant, who has spent the last fifteen years working in the field of business transformation. He has managed both front and back office activities across in-house and commercial organizational development programmes, including systems integration, strategy development, project management, change management, total quality, ISO 9000, process management, Investors in People and a wide range of personal development programmes.

Mick has published widely in the fields of organizational learning, knowledge management, workshop design, change management and personal development and is a regular speaker at international conferences. He is a member of the editorial board of the *Knowledge Management Review* and is an external examiner for Guildhall Business School. He is also the author of *Seven Cs of Consulting* and *Leading the Organisation to Learn*, both published by Financial Times Prentice Hall.

He can be contacted on mick@WizOz.co.uk

Acknowledgements

I would like to thank the following people who helped create and give birth to the ideas in this book.

First of all, Marc Baker for his intellectual challenges during the model design. His skill in helping to design the training programmes, and emotional support and belief in the ideas when I wasn't sure of their market value, were invaluable.

Carmel McConnell for her inspirational ideas, passion, emotional support and contribution to the section on mergers and acquisitions; Ian Marshall for the section on fixed storage; Ingle Dawson for helping with the deconstruction process; Francesca Cerletti for helping me to understand the receivers' point of view. All the team at Catalyst Development who acted as guinea pigs for my early ideas. To Bob Struebig, David Harrison, Theresa Murphy, Peter Moxon, Graham Newbury, Tim Howson, Beatrice Osborn and John Pendle for helping to put real flesh on the model in the early days. To Sara Rowe, Dave Chitty and Sharon Jenkins for listening to my drunken inspirations about the need for change and how the K-Profile will help transform the world! And Rob Chambers for the financial guidance.

To all those people who attended the pilot course and helped to build a more practical and professional K-Profile event. This includes Alison Copley, Maria Schingen, Charles Tucker, Gary Richards, Jeff Brindle, Walter Brady, Sally Pratt, Bowale Sotire, Garry Walsh, John Buckler, Dave Alford, Roland Stainton-Williamson, Chris Middleton, Francesca Cerletti and Steve G. Moore.

Thanks to my editor, Richard Stagg, and Rachael Stock, for having belief in the book and Tony Horsfield for showcasing the early ideas in the FT road shows. Also, Martha Fausset for editing the book and changing my 'less than perfect' English into good sense.

In particular to Professor Peter Woolliams, PhD, Director of Doctoral Programmes, Anglia Business School, who helped me take the first steps down the idea that personal knowledge can be viewed as a stock and flow system.

To, Lin, Michael, Joe, Lucy Cope and Susan Caws for yet again giving me the head, heart and hand space to complete the book – only two more to go. Finally, a special thanks to Gary Porter for yet again giving me time off from the band's (*Crisis Days*) hectic schedule to satisfy my portfolio needs.

Contents

Preface

This book is about choice, the choice to own your own life, your personal capital and your ability to create a market value. I would cite a good friend (Carmel McConnell) who took and lived a difficult choice as part of the Greenham Common peace movement in the 1980s. She suggests that the value of our knowledge is dependent on the extent to which we are prepared to leverage, rather than simply own our personal capital. For her, the knowledge and belief that things needed to change was not sufficient, this knowledge had to be backed up by personal choice and action.

In her speech to court as she was sentenced to 14 days in jail, she said:

> 'it is possible to make a difference (to what happens in life), using will. First of all I had to take responsibility for decisions taken in my name and not let the government have all the control. The proof of whether I really meant it is the action I took.'[1]

I suggest that all the ideas or tools offered in this book pale into insignificance if you do not have the desire to make a choice. To choose to map, measure, manage and market your knowledge. If you don't own and leverage your personal capital then who will?

For information about programmes on the ideas offered in this book, please go to website www.WizOz.co.uk or contact Mick Cope at mick@WizOz.co.uk

Cartoon courtesy of Roger Beale

1

Now it's really personal

Man's main task in life is to give birth to himself, to become what he potentially is. The most important product of his effort is his own personality.

Erich Fromm

Don't you just hate it when your company trots out the standard 'our people are our greatest assets' line and then treat you like a numskull? However, no longer can this bland company slogan be built into the latest vision and values statement without any real intent. The reality is that people *are* the company's greatest asset and the company had better start to realize it. How we think, feel and behave all come together to form our personal capital – our private asset that allows us to trade our knowledge in the market. It is this personal capital that companies increasingly depend upon – and in many cases have to fight to acquire and retain.

Business has changed – whereas it used to be something that revolved around standard pay and reward systems, we are moving towards a world where stock equity is the primary form of reward for contribution to the company. The need to offer stock options to people who were once standard employees has evolved because companies need the rich capital that people bring to them. However, it is this personal aspect that is so critical – this rich asset can walk out the door at any time and as such companies are beginning to develop innovative ways to lock in the personal capital.

No longer can businesses be viewed as cold, impersonal places, where you must walk in the door and switch off your heart and mind. The business world is now intensely personal – because the assets that the business needs can only be found in the capital that you bring to work. But this change in style and emphasis brings new choices and consequences. You can no longer simply walk into work and say 'here you are – take my value and do what you will with it'. Primarily because you cannot always trust these people to realize your full value. In many cases they might well mismanage and devalue your worth through poor investment or maintenance. As such you cannot absolve yourself of responsibility for your personal capital. The essence of your future will be grounded in the exploitation of your capability and this means that you must learn how to map, measure, manage and market your personal capital.

Personal capital

Let's consider this idea of personal capital. Hidden behind the word personal is the deep and challenging idea that we are responsible for the choices we make. Your choice to work for a particular company, take a certain course, accept a certain wage are that – your choice. You cannot say 'I don't earn enough because the company won't pay me', or 'I cannot have the new car that I want because the company has just announced a pay freeze'. In the same way that you make choices about the clothes you wear, the food you eat, or the car you buy, you must now make choices about how to manage your personal capital.

The notion of capital is not something that is generally linked with the word personal. Capital is normally something that companies need to fund investment or use to define their value. However, as we shift to a world where the individual reigns supreme, we must each control our personal capital in the same way that a financial director will jealously lay guard to the financial assets of the business. However, I suggest that very few people – if asked – could say how they truly measure their capitalized value, how much it is worth and how they market it to the world. Instead, so many of us just take the easy way out and let the company tell us what we are worth. When we do that, I suggest that the company will often not understand the value of our capital and will therefore devalue our worth in the market.

A new era

As we move into the knowledge era, all existing economic assumptions and drivers are being ripped apart. Forty years ago people employed in the knowledge and service sector were still less than one-third of the work-force. Now such people account for three-quarters (if not four-fifths) in all developed countries – and this is on the increase.[1]

Knowledge management is not a short-term consulting fad that we can simply disregard. There is a deep cultural and industrial transformation taking place at the heart of every commercial sector around the world. Individuals cannot ignore its coming. Knowledge will be the core com-modity for the foreseeable future and is the factor that will decide how you earn, learn and have fun. This means that you must learn how to learn; must take ownership of your learning processes; and must master how to translate personal knowledge into a marketable asset.

As Charles Handy suggests, you can make more money quickly by selling your expertise and turning it into a product than by selling your time. This is the clue to entrepreneurial success – one that those who live on salaries and wages never discover.[2] As the notion of jobs and wages slowly fades into the background, many of us are faced with Hobson's choice – there is no choice in the matter if we want to survive and prosper in the new millennium. The only choice is that we must learn how to manage our personal capital in the same way we manage our finances, family and free time. The challenge I would make to anyone is: if you do not manage and leverage value from your knowledge, then beware – someone else will!

I believe that the ideas in this book will help you manage your knowledge more effectively. If they do not, then the notion of company-wide know-ledge management is a vague but inspirational dream that will be confined to the archive department along with last year's e-business strategy.

I honestly believe that an organization cannot enhance the value of its collective personal capital solely by the deployment of systems, processes and measures. An organization has two choices. It can take an outside-in approach and try to leverage value out of the collective unit as a whole. Alternatively, it can take the inside-out approach, where individuals are

I honestly believe that an organization cannot enhance the value of its collective personal capital solely by the deployment of systems, processes and measures

helped to understand and enhance the value of their knowledge and consequently increase their personal market value. Once this happens, then it might become possible to facilitate a desire within the individual to apply this personal capital to the benefit of the organization.

Personal capital can be viewed in three primary dimensions. The first dimension is that we hold a stock of knowledge in either explicit or tacit form. The second dimension is the way that we acquire or sell our knowledge as a form of currency. This can be viewed in terms of how we think, behave or feel, or the cognitive, behavioural and affective elements. Finally, as knowledge flows in and out of us we make choices about how it can be processed. The assumption is that at any moment in time we might take a decision to discover, diffuse, deliver, delay or dispose of our knowledge.

By synthesizing these three factors into a single entity, we can develop a pictorial or schematic representation of our knowledge and how it might be deployed. This is called the knowledge profile or K-Profile. This is a simple model that will help any individual take control of his or her personal capital and an organization to manage its personal capital base.

However, I would not suggest that the K-Profile is the answer! My goal is for you to take the issue of personal capital seriously and to start the journey towards developing your own system. As you start to think about such a system, it might be useful to think about some of the following questions:

- What filters do I use that enhance or block my ability to acquire knowledge?
- How do I create new knowledge?
- What investment strategies do I employ that ensure I acquire value added knowledge?
- How effective is my memory as a storage system?
- How do I use systems to store information?
- What impact do emotions have on my storage capability?
- How do I store knowledge in partnership with other people?
- Have I developed my capability to unlearn?
- How do I manage the pain associated with losing knowledge?

- What strategies do I have to ensure that I can modify knowledge on my terms rather than being forced by someone else?
- What explicit and intuitive processes do I use to share and transfer knowledge with colleagues?
- To what extent do competitive forces impact on my ability or desire to share knowledge?
- To what extent do I buy and sell knowledge as a tradable entity?
- How do I use communities of interest to amplify and enhance my personal capital?
- Can I place a market value on my personal capital?
- How do I balance the relationships with my employer and the market?
- Where do I position my personal capital in the market?

These are the foundation questions that have been used to drive and underpin the formation of the K-Profile. I know that there are many more questions that can be asked, but as a starter for ten they have helped me to take a greater degree of control over my life, knowledge and personal capital.

In conclusion, the age of the knowledge individual has arrived with a vengeance. This is because ultimately, learning and knowledge will be discovered and delivered by individuals, not faceless corporate bodies. Hence, if individuals are not motivated to acquire or trade knowledge, then little learning can or will take place at an organizational level. The critical issue is to recognize the significance of the individual's role and value in enhancing the value of personal capital within any modern business.

" The age of the knowledge individual has arrived with a vengeance"

2

The knowledge era

We need to pick up the pace of commercialization. People thought it meant go as fast as you can, instead of learn as fast as you can.

Alan Lafley, CEO, Procter and Gamble

onsider a quiet beach. Three children decide to have a contest. They challenge each other to a game of skipping stones, trying to outdo each other in the goal of achieving the most skips and reaching the farthest distance. John makes a double skip that reaches three metres into the sea. Sara makes four skips and manages to achieve a distance of five metres. Alison steams ahead and manages six skips and reaches a distance of seven metres.

Defining exactly why Alison was able to win is likely to be difficult, but one key component will be the knowledge that she used in throwing the stone. Knowledge gained from watching other children play, from throwing stones in the garden and maybe even from watching a children's show on television. Alison now has two choices. The first is carry on playing the game. The second is to trade her knowledge and, in return for some of their sweets, help the other children develop a similar set of skills.

This simple story offers a powerful example of a new paradigm that is sweeping the world. No longer is knowledge something that is tacitly managed; it is now a tradable commodity with real commercial value on the open market. However, the decisions Alison took at a tacit level now need to be made explicit. You must manage knowledge in the same way you manage time, finances and personal resources. If you do not know the value of your knowledge; the cost of acquiring new skills; or the market demand for capabilities, you will be sidelined to a commodity level within the job market – with a corresponding reduction in your capacity to earn the desired income. You must, therefore, start to understand how and why knowledge management is such an important issue – primarily at a personal rather than corporate level. However, before embarking on this journey, it might make sense to understand what knowledge management is and to consider its background.

The emergence of knowledge management

Knowledge management (KM) has become the hot topic of the new millennium. Books, articles and conferences abound on this topic and people are clamouring to understand how it will impact upon their business and their personal lives. However, much of the published work focuses on the structural aspects of knowledge management: how data is transferred across the organization; how it can be measured and, in particular, the role that technology (in particular intranets) play in its diffusion. There is less consideration of what happens at an individual level. How do people acquire, diffuse and utilize knowledge on a personal level. It is in this area that further work needs to take place and it is in this area that the K-Profile can help you effectively manage your knowledge.

" Knowledge management (KM) has become the hot topic of the new millennium "

Within knowledge management literature, the people element is generally referred to as 'human capital'. This term was first surfaced by Theodore W. Schultz, who argued that the traditional concepts of economics were inadequate for treating the growth prospects of low-income countries. He tried to define the qualitative aspects of capital generation and suggested that the attributes of acquired population quality, which are valuable and can be augmented by appropriate investment, will be treated as human capital.[1] The crucial point made by Schultz is that this asset base does not come for free; it needs investment, nurturing and maintenance. The importance of human capital in the generation of knowledge can be seen in the argument that 'Money talks but it does not think, machines perform, often better than any human beings can, but do not invent.'[2]

From data to capital

Though books, articles and Internet sites abound on the topic of knowledge management, there is little agreement as to the nature of the word 'knowledge', let alone a clear definition of knowledge management. Much of the debate is grounded in the question of its origin, ownership and transferability. Is knowledge a tangible product that can be separated from its owner and hence transferred from person to person? Alternatively, is it something that only exists in the eye of the beholder and is, in essence, a theory of subjective perception? On top of this, there is often confusion over the relationship between data, information, knowledge and personal capital.

However, as with so many other topics in the field of management, there is a danger of veering into the pit of linguistic analysis or philosophical debate in order to arrive at a practical business definition. It is probably impossible to come up with a structural definition that will satisfy everyone, as the whole notion of knowledge and personal capital is in itself a subjective idea. The idea that knowledge can be slotted into a 'data-to-wisdom' hierarchy is bogus, for the simple reason that one person's knowledge is another person's data.[3] However, Fig. 2.1 offers a temporary structure that sets out the relationship between each of the key words.

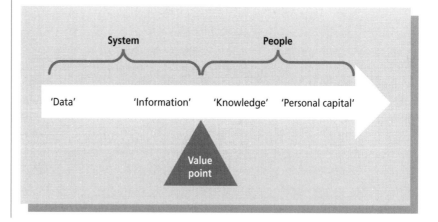

Figure 2.1
Data – personal capital shift

As we interact with the data, we enhance its market value. However, there is a breakpoint where the information becomes knowledge and this is the point where the information enters the human instrument. The owner-ship of knowledge does not automatically lead to market value. We have to make choices – to decide what knowledge can be placed in the open market and how it can be delivered. At this point, innate knowledge becomes an asset and might be viewed as personal capital.

Please note, this is a symbolic framework and should not be seen as a true structural representation of the relationship between data, information and knowledge. Information and knowledge are not always separate en-tities and in many cases will be the same, but viewed from different perspectives.[4] As such it is often difficult, if not impossible, to separate them into discrete entities. This framework is offered as a way to start to understand and structure our personal capital. The danger is that without this guiding structure, we can end up trying to take decisions and choices based on something that is vague, intangible and subjective.

Economic shift

If we are to understand the relationship between information, knowledge, the individual and the company, then it is important to step back and take a broader view of the underlying economic forces that swirl around the market. Clearly, the notion that no man is an island is even more import-ant now than it has been in recent years. Rapid changes in the economy (globalization, pensions and career longevity, etc) all have a direct influ-ence on each one of us. We now see a situation where one person, a PC and an Internet connection can collapse markets, make a million, or flood the world with an electronic virus.

Knowledge economy

In 1917, the number one company in the United States was US Steel Co. Its product was typical of the 'Industrial Age': heavy in weight and light in know-how. In today's terms, it had assets of $30 billion, three times greater than those of the next largest company and employed 268,000 workers. Moving to today's list of the top 100 US companies you will search in vain for the name of US Steel. Its assets are now only $6.5 billion – a fifth of what they were eighty years ago – and it employs a mere 20,800 people. So what kind of companies are making the top 100 list today? Simply those that specialize in intangibles. In the knowledge economy, products don't weigh a ton, they are, instead, the products of the (collective) human mind rather than of the production line. We have moved from the heavyweight to the weightless society.[5]

Historically, as we moved from the agricultural economy to the industrial one; and now as we move from the industrial economy to the knowledge economy, we see a shift in market skills (see Fig. 2.2). For the first shift, people had to transform from working the land to operating in large, centralized units. Now, again, people are being forced to adjust to a changing economy where the emphasis is shifting to the value of their personal capital and how it can be traded in a managed market.

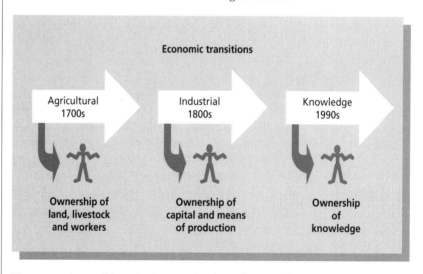

Figure 2.2
Economic transitions

However, the problem is that we don't really understand how knowledge behaves as an economic resource. We have not yet had sufficient experience of the knowledge economy to develop and test theories and extend social and economic guidelines and frameworks.[6] At present a knowledge-based economy does not behave in the way that existing theory might suggest.

Much of this might be because of the seismic shift in the ownership of knowledge. In the industrial age, people were content to become corporate slaves, and in doing so gave up much of their personal freedom in exchange for a living wage and job security. In doing this they often gave up their right to own and sell their personal knowledge. With the shift to the knowledge era we see people rescinding their commitment to corporate slavery and in turn take back their right to manage their personal knowledge. Now people think twice before offering a great new idea to their employer and instead toy with the idea that maybe they should take it to market themselves. As such, the firm's traditional source of market wealth is slowly slipping from its grasp and in many cases the senior managers don't understand either the economic implication or how to resolve the problem.

Whose knowledge is it anyway?

With the migration to a personal capital-based economy, it becomes clear that the whole notion of knowledge, power and ownership can be questioned. As you become more attuned to the idea of knowledge ownership, so you will start to understand the degree of power associated with your specific knowledge base. This will lead to a shift in the spoken and unspoken control structure within your firm. The result might well be a shift in the underlying language constructs, as the notion of worker and boss becomes obsolete. The notion of working *for* someone, although likely to continue, will start to be erased as you realize the power your knowledge offers.

Along with this we see a shift from highly bureaucratic structures to more open and network-based organizations. We now see flatter, thinner and leaner work structures that place greater emphasis on the value of an individual's personal capital, as opposed to their actual position in the company. The consequence is that the work relationship is shifting from one of paternalistic dependence to open-interdependence. This gentle shift can be seen in the way that many companies now strive to achieve internal coordination and collaboration rather than control and containment.

So, as this new world unfolds, we see before us tremendous opportunities for growth, personal gain and business expansion. However, there is a flaw in the idea because all of the baseline assumptions rest on the will and capability of the human being. The whole notion of knowledge management is predicated on the idea that knowledge will be shared when people are faced with a shiny screen and a fat bonus. The reality is far from this! People are cautious, suspicious and in many cases choose not to share knowledge even when it offers benefits to them personally.

Therefore, I suggest that companies are potentially wasting millions of pounds by implementing knowledge systems that will not deliver the required business improvement. Consider the two words independently. First, 'knowledge' is generally accepted as something that sits between the ears and behind the eyes, whereas information is deemed to be something that is outside the individual and can be manipulated as a tangible entity. Second, the word 'management' is defined as the process of taking control, organizing or directing a person or situation. As such, the notion of knowledge management is actually a synthesis of two-management disciplines, the science of information management and the art of people management.

Herein lies the paradox, look at any journal, web site or business article and knowledge management is often associated with technology, in particular the implementation of in-house intranet systems. Look again and you will see scant reference to the role of the individual in the process of knowledge creation. This is akin to an architect presenting a fantastic plan to build a new town but forgetting that a town is not a set of buildings, but a place where people live. It is this type of approach that contributed to the planning problems for the new towns of the 1960s and it is this type of approach that will contribute to the installation of barren intranets and networks.

If it's not personal – it's not real

In the Industrial Age many jobs were for life and the corporate apron strings were rarely severed; careers took care of themselves; and the company adopted the role of nurturing parent. Nowadays, the relationship between employees and organizations is in flux. It is being challenged by trends such as increasing individualism (free agents), the rise of the truly global organization and the rapidly growing opportunities caused by innovative information and communication technologies.

As a result we are witnessing a major re-think in the way that capital is managed within a business. The most visible shift is the migration from a focus on financial and physical capital, to the expert management of human capital. As Ed Michael, a director of McKinsey and Co, suggests, 'capital is accessible, smart strategies can simply be copied and the half life of technology is growing shorter all the time – so people are the prime source of competitive advantage'.

However, as you take on the mantra of a knowledge worker you must also accept that your knowledge is only as current as today's newspaper. As demand changes so the market shifts and so will your knowledge account. The reality is that the workers of the future will have to routinely change careers, possibly every seven to ten years during their working lives. These changes are likely to be even more traumatic than the initial shock of moving from the educational systems to work. This will even be evident in those industries that are at the forefront of a move towards a knowledge structure. Consider stockbrokers, travel agents and estate agents. All these people are primarily employed to manage the transfer of information. However, as technology opens up new brokerage systems, so their roles will diminish in their current form and probably migrate to a new style of working where they add a different type of value to the information exchange. If this is the case, then it leads to a further complication – that of a shift in the typical career plan.

Consider the traditional life pattern that people follow. It is often built around the idea of a four-act play: childhood, study years, work years and retirement. This life pattern has been entrenched, yet it is coming under attack as we shift towards a knowledge world.

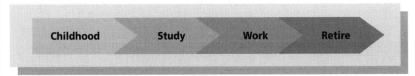

Figure 2.3
Traditional life structure

The shift to a knowledge-based economy demands that traditional relationships between education, learning and work are fundamentally reappraised. The long-running debate over whether and to what extent education should be a preparation for work as well as life is being overtaken by events, with work and learning being increasingly interrelated, integrated and interdependent. No longer can professionals sit back and expect their years of hard work to provide an income for the rest of their life. They will need to plan for personal capital refresh periods, when, as a minimum, they update their knowledge base and in some cases even consider a total transformation of their career structure. Therefore, the career structure of the knowledge worker will be iterative rather than linear in nature.

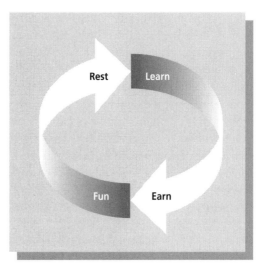

Figure 2.4
New life structure

Additionally, companies can no longer expect their employees to build their knowledge capability based on the job function they are performing at that moment in time. There must be a shift towards an equitable balance in the knowledge that individuals want to acquire and that which companies want them to gain. Quite simply, if you are not energized and in tune with the idea of learning and knowledge creation, then little is likely to happen. However, developing people who are able and happy to embrace this view of life is not something that can be mandated or casually rolled out in a corporate programme. No longer will people accept that their life patterns should be one of school, work and retirement; no longer is the single employer for life a given factor; and no longer is it a fact that work takes precedence over the home. A key success factor for companies in the future will be their capability to balance organizational business needs with employees' personal needs.[8]

However, trying to implement a personal knowledge system is not something that can be mandated. Consider the consulting firm in the Netherlands which installed a database on its intranet to house the curricula vitae (CVs) of its people. Consultants were asked to fill in their data in both Dutch and English and to keep it current. The chairperson of the Board then sent a directive saying that the consultants were required to give information about their educational background and work experience and the Board would be regularly informed about each individual's participation. One month later, the chairperson sent out a harshly worded memo demanding cooperation. Three months later, only 20% of the consultants had filled in their details despite this top-down, force and control approach. This once again proves that you can lead consultants to water, but cannot force them to drink.[9]

Only by developing inclusive strategies can the organization start to understand the complex relationship that exists between individual learning, organizational learning and knowledge management. As Peter Senge suggests, 'Organizations learn only through individuals who learn. Individual learning does not guarantee organizational learning, but without it, no organizational learning occurs.'[10]

Manage your knowledge – or someone else will

Consider, over the latter part of the last century, how different management principles emerged and combined into a professional discipline. Of all the skills that a professional is expected to hold, time management is somewhere to the fore. This personal discipline can be seen to blossom, even from school. As children we are forced into the discipline of blocks of time at school; at college, one of the first guiding rules offered by the tutor is about the need to manage study time; and at work, some people now micro-manage themselves down to the minute. In this rush to manage time, where is the desire to manage knowledge? I suggest that it is generally subordinate to time in terms of importance. However, I can create a greater market value by selling one hour's worth of knowledge than I can one hour of my physical time.

Step back in time 20 years and the notion that you might attend a time management course as part of your personal development might have been deemed crazy, costly and unnecessary. However, as the value of time increased, so companies came to recognize that people have to be trained how to use time more effectively. Towards the end of the twentieth century, Ashridge Strategic Management Centre introduced its first time management programme after delegates started to mention that time management was a personal problem.[11] Time had become a critical factor in the way that individuals, teams and organizations managed themselves. Now most companies either run in-house time management programmes or invest quite heavily in external programmes to help people manage their time.

In the same way that it has become accepted that people need to manage their time to become effective, so knowledge management should be seen to be just as important. We must shift to a stage where knowledge management courses – programmes where people are taught how to map, measure, manage and market their personal capital – are valued as of critical importance.

Knowledge is now as critical as time and in many cases more important. As we move to a knowledge-based economy, so the pressure will be for you to manage knowledge more effectively. To the point where the capability to effectively process knowledge at an individual level will provide a commercial differentiator for the company. This leads to the conclusion that, in the same way that people who use them own their time management systems, we need to develop a business ethos where people also create and manage a personal capital system.

Choice and consequences

Knowledge management is ultimately about choice – choice of which paper to read, which book to borrow from the library, which Internet site to browse, or which product to take to market.

To consider the idea of knowledge choice, we must first consider those factors that help an individual make a reasoned decision. For any given choice, it is necessary for all the alternative options to be known and for the outcomes or consequences of those choices to be recognized by the individual. This is a situation sometimes known as the condition of perfect knowledge. Second, in order to maximize the process, the decision maker must have available a mechanism that will allow priorities to be assigned based upon the desirability or value of the outcome. Therefore, we must be able to consider the merits of all the alternatives open in a particular decision in order to choose the one that will offer most value in the market. Finally, these decisions must be taken against a set of values or criteria that make sense to us at a personal level. This is known as the condition of perfect judgement.[12]

Where you make critical decisions about your knowledge, then the baseline is that three conditions need to be satisfied:

- options (including known impact)
- prioritization criteria
- personal values.

Knowledge options often need to be considered across a wide spectrum. Consider the individual who has an hour free every morning as he travels into work on the train. The first thing he has to consider is what are the knowledge options. Does he read the paper, write the management report that is due the following week, read his son's school report, or update his diary? These are all knowledge options that need to be managed. The first step might be to clarify the options along with the impact they might have. Once the options are understood, he or she can then make a decision against a set of known criteria. This might be time based (which one is due first?); delivery based (can it be managed on the train?); or impact based (which one will give the best return against the time invested?). None of these questions can be answered unless he has a clear sense of value associated with each one.

When faced with a work/home life conflict, the danger is that confusion and guilt sets in, such that more time is spent being frustrated about not being able to write the management report and read the school report. The solution is to have a clear set of personal values that guide how important things and people are, so that knowledge time can be fairly allocated to each area.

This example highlights two points.

● Knowledge is as valuable a commodity as time and so needs to be managed with as much care and attention.

● Knowledge choice is not necessarily confined to the business world.

We all operate as stakeholder units or stakeholder collectives with many different people and demands influencing our knowledge decisions.[13] As such, the knowledge choice might aim to be one with a perfect outcome, but in reality, the different goals that drive each of the roles in a personal life will possibly force a choice of minimum rather than maximum satisfaction. This is often termed as satisficing, which is a choice taken on the limited worldview that we all have to live with.[14] However, I would argue that individuals who choose to own and manage their knowledge, rather than let it be managed for them will automatically be more effective.

Knowledge does not appear all at once. Rather, it accumulates slowly over time and is shaped and channelled into certain directions through the nudging of hundreds of daily managerial decisions. These knowledge reservoirs are not static pools but wellsprings, constantly replenished with streams of new ideas and constituting an ever-flowing source of renewal.[15] Inspired people will recognize how important it is to manage this flow and stock of knowledge for themselves and the organizations they work for.

" Few people realize that knowledge is a stock that has to be continually refreshed and renewed"

The problem is that few people realize that knowledge is a stock that has to be continually refreshed and renewed. This renewal process is one that has to be thought about every second of the day. Every time we read a paper, deliver a lecture, or teach our children how to play with a ball, we take choices about the knowledge we hold and offer to the world. The suggestion is that the K-Profile offers a simple but structured framework that will help you take a greater degree of control over the knowledge acquisition and deployment processes.

The underlying message is that the balance of power is shifting from the organization to the individual. We see a transference of ownership whereby individuals now have the choice about what knowledge they acquire and deploy. With the range of information that rests at the fingertips of all workers, they can no longer offer excuses that they are unable to change their lives because of the culture, government, political systems, etc (select any one at random). Individuals now have the choice to manage their knowledge growth and so manage their acquisition of power. The K-Profile is offered as a simple tool (not a solution) that will help you join this worldwide transformation.

3

Shadow knowledge

Power always has to be kept in check; power exercised in secret, especially under the cloak of national security, is doubly dangerous.

William Proxmire

hadow knowledge is one of the great unspoken problems associated with knowledge management. It is one of the things that brings the mighty consulting machine to a halt and stymies all attempts to transform a company's performance. No matter how much time, energy and money a company invests in new information systems, unless you are prepared to share that hidden piece of information you value, then little improvement in knowledge sharing will be realized.

Knowledge can exist in two forms: surface knowledge, that which is in the open and used in the public domain; and shadow knowledge, that which is hidden from normal view. It is the tension between these two forms that can block the process of knowledge diffusion, as people and teams struggle to reconcile the gap between that which is open and discussable and that which sits below the surface.

A story about the Rank Xerox technical representatives can help illustrate the point. In developing a new system, the company sent a researcher to travel with field technicians. When problems with copiers arose, the researcher asked to see the manuals the field technicians consulted. Early on, before they got comfortable with the researcher, the field technicians would pull out the 'official' company manual which was clean, pristine, neatly organized. Over time, though, they started showing the researcher their 'real' manual. It was the standard book, but highlighted, dog-eared, filled with scribbles in the margins and annotated with notes and reminders.

Each technician was keeping two sets of books: the formal and the informal, the official and the improvized. But isn't that true for work in general? Each of us, in our own way, keeps two sets of books. And too often, what is unofficial remains invisible – except perhaps to members of our own trusted community. In the knowledge era, what's invisible is often what's most valuable.[1]

Although we might design an organization around people, roles and markets, the reality is that you will take on different styles and thoughts dependent upon how you fit within your world. As William James suggested, whenever two people meet there are actually six people present. There is each man as he sees himself, each man as the other person sees him and each man as he really is. In the same way, when an individual uses information within an organization, there can be a range of interpretations of the information and its use. Some information the organization views as important but is not viewed as such by the individual; some the individual thinks is of value, but is ignored by the organization; and some neither side views as important, but can be of significance for the business.

A summary definition of shadow knowledge might be taken as all the important information that does not get identified, discussed and managed in formal decision-making forums. The shadow side deals with the covert, the undiscussed, the undiscussable and the unmentionable.[2] These sit in the shade of the person or organization and only appear when a light is deliberately shone upon them. Hence, this offers four separate areas that can be opened up for consideration: the open and hidden individual and the open and hidden organization:

" The shadow side deals with the covert, the undiscussed, the undiscussable and the unmentionable "

Open organization	Open individual
Hidden organization	Hidden individual

Figure 3.1
Shadow knowledge table

This was considered in a famous case study by Janis on the formation of groupthink within teams.[3] His study considered the Bay of Pigs fiasco that occurred during the early stage of John F. Kennedy's presidential term. The primary goal behind the Bay of Pigs invasion was to train a secret army of Cuban exiles to invade Cuba and fight Castro. The attack was a disaster from the start with the conclusion that, within three days, all the surviving members of the brigade were in prison camps. When the attack failed, Kennedy was stunned. 'How,' he asked, 'could I have been so stupid to let them go ahead?' The problem was driven primarily by the notion of groupthink, where a team makes a collective decision that is less than ideal.

This situation occurs when the group creates an illusionary schema around itself, one that is not in alignment with the real world. However, as well as developing this shared schema, the group also creates a number of powerful defence mechanisms that block anyone from questioning the reality of the frame of reference.[4] While each member of the group might individually recognize the apparent disconnection between how the group think and reality, the barriers are such that they are either unable or unwilling to surface the issue.

Interestingly, after the Bay of Pigs, one of the cabinet members wrote, 'I bitterly reproached myself for having kept so silent during those critical discussions in the cabinet room.' He suggests that part of the reason he didn't challenge the accepted wisdom is because of a fear of being seen as a nuisance. This is a clear example of the existence of surface and shadow knowledge affecting the knowledge management process. Clearly each of the members had his or her own shadow knowledge, but because of social pressure, power issues or general malaise, he or she failed to bring it to the surface.

The existence of this shadow information can also be seen in a business environment and in many cases to devastating effect. There are many stories that describe how a company can lose the ability to see the market as it really is: IBM's inability to accept the rise of the minicomputer which led to it being undermined by Digital Equipment Corporation (who were themselves undercut by the rise of the PC); Wang's loss of market share as it failed to predict the rise of the word-processing market on PCs; Microsoft's inability to see how the Internet would take the PC market by storm. In all of these cases there were people within the organizations aware of the impending changes in the market, but unable or unwilling to diffuse this knowledge. As such the companies managed the knowledge that they wanted to see, rather than what they needed to see.

A clear example of this dissonance is offered by Andrew Grove, chairman of the Intel Corporation. He described how at one critical stage in the company's growth, the senior team was intensely focused on the ongoing development of the company as a memory producer. However, the company's middle managers had executed a strategic turn and diverted resources into the emerging microprocessor business. This was not because of any specific strategic direction by the senior team, but because of daily decisions by the production and finance managers who actually ran the business. He suggests that many companies fall into this trap of saying one thing and doing another. He calls the divergence between actions and statements strategic dissonance.[5] This is one of the surest indications that shadow knowledge is being utilized and people are not doing what they say they are doing.

Shadow knowledge often exists because the company tries to protect itself from pain. Managers make the choice to use knowledge that will allow them to look favourable in the current climate, rather than surfacing issues that might lead to confrontation and upheaval. This is similar to the coping mechanisms that people in the emergency services develop to protect themselves from emotional pain. If we consider the emotional anxiety and stress that these people go through every day, they clearly have to develop the ability to separate themselves from the emotional pain and operate in a detached way. In the same way, managers often develop the capability to disassociate themselves from the bad news that starts to emerge as problems develop within an organization.

As organizations follow this pattern they subconsciously filter out the information that signals problems and instead choose to selectively filter in the data that reinforces their view that everything is fine. This results in four separate knowledge sets as seen in Fig. 3.2.

Open organization	Open individual
Reports and accounts	Personal objectives
Espoused ethos and ideals	Team goals
Company values	Personal plans
Product data	Team briefs
Market data	Monthly reports
Formal communication	Casual conversations
Planned strategy	Yearly appraisal
Hidden organization	**Hidden individual**
Failed projects	True personal goals
Local custom and practice	Personal relationships
Race, gender or religious data	Mistakes made
Backstage decision making	Feelings about manager
Informal networks	Historic problems with company
Emergent business strategies	
Shadow organization structure	

Figure 3.2
Surface and shadow knowledge

However, being aware of the existence of shadow knowledge and moving it to the surface are different matters. Often, the organization's immune system becomes highly effective at resisting bad news and in many cases actively chastises any individual or team that tries to bring it to the surface.

In his recent book, Bill Gates stresses the need to surface this shadow knowledge by helping the bad news to travel fast. He says 'I have a natural instinct for hunting down grim news. If it's out there I want to know about it.' The essential quality of a good manager is a determination to deal with any kind of bad news head on – to seek it out rather than deny it. However, it is a rare organization that adopts and actually lives this philosophy. Unfortunately, the large majority of organizations that aspire to manage their information more effectively will operate the 'sweep it under the carpet' approach, where shadow information is hidden away in the archives for later generations of managers to unearth.

"Often, the organization's immune system becomes highly effective at resisting bad news"

The underlying factor that drives all these strategies is the dependence on the individual, the notion that someone understands that shadow knowledge exists; that it can be harmful; and that it can only be managed by pulling it to the surface. However, here lies the dilemma. Before it is accepted that shadow knowledge can be managed, we must first accept the notion that we own and manage our knowledge and understand how it can be managed. If people don't accept that they own shadow knowledge, then what chance is there that they will take responsibility for surfacing issues that cause problems for the business?

As such, the account manager who tacitly realizes that a major client is losing market share must understand how this affects the business as a whole and not just his or her personal bonus for that month. The company that can surface this type of shadow data stands a chance to leverage real competitive advantage by overriding obsolete data. The company that continues to manage only the superficial surface knowledge might well be made obsolete by a competitor.

Although the fact that people are unwilling to share knowledge might be viewed as a political situation, it might well be something altogether different. In reality it might be a negotiation issue. If someone asks to borrow money from a bank, then the first thing they do is check against their capital holding to ensure that funds are available. On the basis that they have sufficient funds and the loan can be repaid with interest, the loan will go ahead. In the same way, when an organization wants to encourage knowledge sharing within the business, it asks you to invest your personal capital in other people. If this is the case, then it behoves the organization to first help you understand what knowledge resides in your personal account and from this consider how you might wish to share it with colleagues.

It might be that you resist sharing knowledge because you do not have a clear appreciation of the value of your personal capital. If this is the case, then it would be natural to resist letting go, since it might be the last knowledge dollar left in your bank. If however, you understand what personal stocks you have in the bank and how you could increase the asset base by sharing them with others, you might be willing to spread the value across the business. In this case, the notion of shadow knowledge might be diminished if people do not feel the need to bottle up and hide their personal capital. The primary argument is that shadow knowledge often exists because of the unknown rather than any premeditated notion to subsume personal knowledge.

Unless you understand how to acquire, store and utilize knowledge, then it is far too easy for personal capital to be locked away in a shadow container, only to be used as a political tool in times of desperation. Although this can realize powerful short-term benefit, I suggest that in the long term it will lead to the view that you use your knowledge for duplicitous and selfish reasons. So, I suggest that you have to make quite significant choices about your personal knowledge and the extent to which you want it to operate from the surface or shadow arena.

4

The K-Profile™

Real knowledge is to know the extent of one's ignorance.

Confucius

If you truly wish to understand how to place a value on what you know, then the first step is to understand and map what you don't know. You must step back three paces and build a map that defines and describes your entire personal capital. One that will describe how you acquire, store, delete, share and sell your personal assets. This is where use of the Knowledge Profile or K-Profile can help to define that which you know you know, that which you know you don't know and also identify personal assets that you have totally ignored.

However, to take this action, we might need to look at the world in a different way. Whereas many advances in the field of knowledge management focus on the idea of knowledge creation and distribution, it may be time to step up a level and help individuals gain knowledge about their knowledge. To shift from a view of 'know-how' and 'know-what' to one that considers personal knowledge from the perspective of know-why and know-when.

So often we fall into the content and context trap. We assume that because it is possible to use knowledge to create a market value today, this will continue. Now, with the rampant change in industry, both the content and context of our knowledge might need to change on a yearly basis. When we have the luxury to operate in a predictable world, then it is possible to maintain an income by responding to the market. In an era of discontinuity and unpredictability, there is greater pressure for people to adopt a market leadership role, to take personal responsibility for mapping where the market might head and to develop the appropriate competencies to operate in such a market.

The K-Profile is a framework that will help you resolve this situation. It offers a simple but powerful system to define how knowledge can be managed. The system has three core components:

● **knowledge stock** – how knowledge is stored;

● **knowledge currency** – how you acquire and offer knowledge to the market;

● **knowledge flow** – how knowledge passes from discovery to delivery.

As these three knowledge factors are synthesized, so a detailed K-Profile can be constructed, one that offers a fully comprehensive model to help you manage your personal capital, as seen in Fig. 4.1.

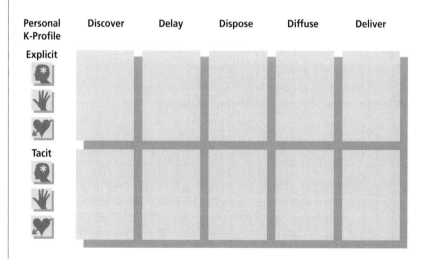

Figure 4.1
K-Profile

In the following chapters, I consider a number of ideas. First each of the three ideas of knowledge stock, currency and flow are explored in more detail. I then consider what process you might follow to build your K-Profile. Finally, I start to explore some of the different ways that the K-Profile can be used to enhance your value as well as your business's value.

However, it is important to highlight that the K-Profile is not being offered as a robust scientific model that describes the process we all follow to manage knowledge. Like all personal effectiveness systems, it is a symbolic representation of a highly complex model – and one that we have yet to really understand. It is offered on the basis that the first step to making any process effective is to develop a simple process map – one that sets out a high-level view of the way that units come into and leave the business. The K-Profile offers a simple view of the way that we acquire and distribute our personal capital. Only you can understand how best to manage your personal capital – but the K-Profile will help you reach the stage where you have a greater degree of leverage and control.

" The K-Profile is not being offered as a robust scientific model that describes the process we all follow to manage knowledge"

5

K-Profile elements

What is not fully understood is not possessed.
Johann Wolfgang Von Goethe

Knowledge stock

We can think of knowledge as something stored at two levels. The first and most obvious is that which we are able to describe, overtly codify and explicitly manage. The second and more interesting is the tacit level – things that an individual is able to do, but not to describe how they do it.

- **Explicit** – knowledge that can be codified and readily expressed.
- **Tacit** – knowledge that is difficult to express.

Explicit

Explicit knowledge is that which can be expressed in words and numbers and can be easily communicated and shared in the form of hard data, scientific formulae, codified procedures or universal principles.[1] This is the hard and tangible knowledge that can be codified, replicated and readily transferred across an organization. It is the stuff we find in books, reports, newspapers and safety instructions that are announced on the railway. The use of explicit knowledge will have the following effects.

- It will make internal models public. Once explicit, the knowledge can be readily communicated and shared with others. This enables a greater degree of speed and flexibility than knowledge which is held inside and uncoded. For example, the fact that I work with people who all use the same client management system means that we enhance our ability to share information and our capacity to respond to client enquires more efficiently.

● It will help define open rules and regimes. Once something is explicit, it can take on the form of a direction or rule. The growth in business process management was often driven by the elicitation of deep tacit knowledge into hard codified process and rules that could be applied across the company.

● It will enable a shift in ownership and power. The moment I can explain how to produce a particular sound on the bass guitar it makes it easier for the band to kick me out and get in someone else who is younger, slimmer and better looking. Hence, I might choose to hold onto this secret rather than share it with other members of the band.

● It will facilitate the measurement process. Once something is explicit, then it becomes easier for an objective viewer to measure the internal performance. If someone is delivering a service but cannot describe how, then all that can be measured is the input and output stage. Once the process is made explicit, it becomes possible to measure and investigate how effectively the internal transactions are operating.

● It's possible to protect its intellectual value. Once made explicit and codified, it becomes possible to patent and protect the knowledge. If you are unable to describe the process in a codified form then there is nothing stopping someone else from replicating the product and selling it to the market. Once you have been able to describe it in detail, the knowledge can be patented. In the case of the inventor and scientist, it is the patenting process that enables them to reap the value of their personal capital.

However, just because knowledge has been made explicit it doesn't mean that it will always be effective. If an individual's knowledge is articulated within an organization, the ability of individuals outside that organization to understand the full meaning of the articulated knowledge cannot be presumed.[2] So often explicit knowledge is actually grounded in the context where it originated. So engineers will create explicit knowledge that is actually based upon tacit engineering inferences and assumptions. The same applies to marketing, personnel and operational people. As a result, it is not always possible to simply transplant people from one operational unit into another on the assumption that behaviours can be transferred. The high level of failures in corporate mergers and acquisition is a sad testimony to this idea.

One area where this often surfaces (and fails) is in the notion of best practice. While the idea that we should learn from the experience of others is valid and of immense benefit, I can only explicitly see and observe what you learnt, I cannot feel what you felt, therefore it is difficult for me to really absorb the deep and rich experience that you went through. Often the explicit knowledge is grounded in a tacit experience and hence cannot be readily transferred.

Tacit

Tacit knowledge is the informal, hard-to-pin-down ability. It is in the fingertips or muscle capability – where you can perform a task but find it difficult to explain. It can be the knowledge that you don't recognize that you have, e.g. how to open a door may not seem like 'knowledge' until you meet somebody who's never seen a door. One simple way to describe tacit knowledge is in the phrase 'we can know more than we can tell'. Another way to describe it is 'the answer to questions that haven't been asked yet'.[3] Whatever definition is used, it is fundamentally about that which we apply and use, but have yet to codify in such a way that we can describe how we perform that action.

Tacit knowledge has received a great deal of attention because it is recognized, as valuable to both the individual and organization. However, because of its nature it is difficult to codify or store. Look at individuals; ask them to describe what they do and how they do it. The guarantee is that you will only gain a partial appreciation of their unique skills and knowledge. The tacit element is that knowledge that they are probably unable to describe. Ask musicians to explain how they get a unique sound; sports people how they get that extra inch; or police detectives how they catch criminals. All of these elements are buried deep within the individual and as such it can be difficult to transform this deep knowledge into a codified form.

It is for this very reason that tacit knowledge is highly prized by many companies. By building a competitive position around its tacit knowledge base, it ensures that any competitor will find it difficult to replicate its market offering. Therefore tacit knowledge is likely to be more a source of competitive advantage than the articulated or non-tacit knowledge.[4] However, the moment we make our tacit capability explicit it can be replicated by another person or company and offered in the market. Hence, in many cases it might be to the company's disadvantage to codify its tacit knowledge because, in the process of making it explicit, it can be copied by the competitors.

Tacit knowledge is highly prized by many companies

In many cases we are unaware that we have a particular tacit structure until it is challenged.[5] As one footballer watches another, he or she might pick up hints and tricks without consciously changing his or her mental models on how to tackle, pass or shoot. This is often referred to as *knowing in action* and can be seen to have the following properties.

● There are actions, recognitions and judgements that we know how to carry out spontaneously; we do not have to think about them prior to or during their performance.

● We are often unaware of having learnt to do these things; we simply find ourselves doing them.

Tacit knowledge is often learned through extended periods of experiencing and doing a task, during which the individual develops a feel for and a capacity to make intuitive judgements about the activity. Machine operators, photocopier repair technicians, ship navigators, bank account officers, doctors and managers are but a few examples of professionals where tacit knowledge plays an instrumental role. Tacit knowledge is vital to the organization because organizations can only learn and innovate by somehow leveraging the implicit knowledge of their members. The most advanced computer-based information systems on their own do not generate new knowledge only human beings, led by tacit knowledge, have the capability to do so.[6]

It is important to understand that the stock model offers a very simplistic representation of two forms of knowledge (explicit and tacit). This is not to suggest that they are actually held or used separately by an individual. It would be very difficult to use explicit knowledge of something unless it is directed by a tacit understanding of 'how to'. It would also be difficult to use the 'how to' or tacit skills unless they are framed through an explicit view of the world. They are mutually interdependent and cannot be managed separately. What the model does offer is a simple framework by which you can start to understand the differences and, more importantly, understand where focus might be placed when you wish to acquire or sell knowledge.

For example, imagine that I want to improve my capability to play a particular style of jazz. Now jazz is not very easy to play because it is often driven by freeform improvization and interplay with other musicians. So, in trying to develop this capability, I can plan the improvement on two levels. One is to enhance my explicit understanding of the theoretical structure of jazz and to develop the skills needed to play a style. The second level might be to consider how I develop a tacit ability and this will be through close association with other musicians. This way I can learn by copying and mimicking their style, almost at an unconscious level. Although the explicit and tacit changes are interdependent, I can choose to manage how they grow and what focus I place on each area.

Knowledge currency

Consider the human instrument as something that interfaces with the world. As we interact with the environment we make different types of exchanges. We take in oxygen and give out carbon dioxide; we take in food and water and give out waste to be reprocessed; we take in money in exchange for our effort and then pass this on to someone as part of a negotiated exchange process. I suggest that we also follow a similar pattern with knowledge. We take in information from other people or things, process it, possibly add some value and then sell that knowledge in return for some personal benefit.

So at this point of interconnect with the world, we trade knowledge almost as a form of soft currency. We pay money to read someone else's book and take in their information; we attend a course to gain skills; or we pay to see a play that will uplift our spirit or give us insight into someone else's emotional view of the world.

Once we have acquired this knowledge, we might store it for later use, or trade it in exchange for some other piece of information that takes our fancy. So, after you read the latest book by Tom Peters, you might use his ideas in a business presentation that in turn earns you respect within the company. After attending a course you use your new skills to negotiate a sale with a client. The macho manager uses the emotional insight he got from a play to build a better relationship with the women on his project team. All of these are knowledge trades, where we have taken ideas, skills or emotions from the outside world and then used or bartered them in exchange for another form of income.

If we look at these examples, they fall into three-currency groups. We can exchange knowledge with the world in terms of how we think (cognitive), act (behave) or feel (affect). In the K-Profile, three symbolic names or icons are used to represent these currencies as shown below.

 Head represents the thought element;

 Hand indicates how we act, behave or physically interact with the world;

 Heart is used to indicate the emotions that we use to manage ourselves and our relationships with others.

It is important to stress that the distinction between these three currency areas is not offered with hard delineations. At first sight the action undertaken by a car mechanic might be seen as trading his behavioural skills for a return in the market. However, a large component of his work will be driven by what he knows, especially with modern cars where an appreciation of the system software is in many ways more important than the ability to wield a wrench. Finally, would you sooner have your car fixed by someone who cares about their work, or are you happy to leave it to someone who is unhappy, emotionally run down and generally not very in tune with your personal needs?

In the vast majority of cases we draw upon all three currencies to create value in the market. However, although all three might be used to deliver a single product, it is likely that one of them will take a dominant role. So, as a musician, my dominant factor is a hand currency because my added value comes from the skills of playing the guitar. As an author, the dominant factor is head currency because you are getting my ideas and mental tools. Finally, much of my market value as a consultant comes from the heart currency and my ability to create an effective emotional relationship with the client. Now this isn't to suggest that the people who watch me play in the local bar don't value my emotions as I play or my ability to know what notes to play. The core added value is around the capability to play the bass guitar and the other currencies help position that in the market.

Head

Thomas Jefferson once said, 'If two individuals get together and exchange a dollar, they each walk away with a dollar. If the same individuals get together and exchange an idea, they both walk away with two ideas.' In many ways, this statement indicates the need to understand the cognitive element of knowledge management. Cognition, the basic unit of the mental framework, is the act of knowing and processing information.

This act of knowledge and processing can be split into many areas including the following.

- Problem diagnostics and interpretation, which is the ability to discriminate between factors and take the appropriate decision based upon the evidence.

- Numerical or verbal ability, which might be seen as the capability to understand and arrange ideas according to a certain set of patterns and rules.

- Visual or spatial interpretation, or the ability to perceive and visualize objects in space.

In essence, our cognitive ability is often viewed as our intelligence or general mental ability. It refers to our capability to process information and to use such information to manage our behaviour. This capability is not limited to a few of the more common intellectual areas that are normally included in the bracket of intelligence. Whereas most intelligence tests have focused on the ability to reason and calculate, there are many other forms of intelligence that we need to consider when thinking about the head element.[7] One Harvard professor suggests that we have many types of intelligence, including linguistic, logical, musical, kinaesthetic, visual, spatial, interpersonal and intrapersonal. This highlights the need to really understand how we mentally process things and more importantly how we use these mental processes to create market value for ourselves.

Ultimately, we all have to understand and take control of two head issues: how to acquire new ideas and information from the outside world and how to deliver this in exchange for income or personal gain. It is in this simple exchange of ideas, beliefs and intellectual creation that we enhance our personal capital and hence our capability to trade with the world.

Hand

Hand is a generic term covering acts, activities, responses, reactions, movements, processes, operations, etc. In short, it is any measurable response of an organism.[8] This might be seen as knowledge that is visible to an observer, can be described by the owner and is delivered using a tangible capability. This might be a sportsperson's ability to score goals or break records, a manager's ability to lead a team, or the way that a mechanic is able to repair the bodywork of a damaged car.

If we look at behaviour as a currency to be exchanged and bartered in the world, we might look at the transaction process. We can start to ask questions such as: How do I acquire my skills and behaviours? How do I know what skills are worth acquiring? How do I create a market for my skills? What value should I place on my ability to perform a function for someone else. We can start to see the process of acquisition and delivery as a buy/sell process. We buy new skills by attending a course; we in turn add to our personal value and experience; and then sell it to the market for a higher rate?

The key issue to consider at this stage is what your hand assets are. So often we might pick up our CV and list the various competencies and skills that are currently on offer to the market. My assertion is that all this does is to list those skills that you are conscious that you sell. In many cases you might have skills and experience that can be sold on the market, but forget that they exist. So many times, when deconstructing someone's K-Profile, I've found that people offer one of their skills as a manager in a particular function and assume that is their primary skill. Only by deconstructing this to a lower level of fragmentation am I able to pull out the real skills and behaviours they use to create a value. These often consist of:

● the ability to negotiate with peers, suppliers and customers;

● the capability to motivate teams of people in difficult situations;

● years of experience in dealing with conflict;

● problem management;

● project management.

These are all highly prized market capabilities that people wrap into a vague and simplistic one-line statement that at best offers a restricted view of their value and at worst destroys potential market worth for any future customer base. If you want to understand the value of your personal capital, then you must understand in some detail how you create market value and not just accept the vague job titles that are given in the workplace.

● Heart

An individual can acquire knowledge through emotional interaction with other people. Although some might link it into the softer aspects of learning, such as counselling, caring and artistic creativity, Daniel Goldman has brought it to the forefront of the knowledge arena with his debate on the importance of emotional intelligence.[9]

Heart knowledge can be defined in the following ways.

● Being able to resolve situations by dealing with others in an open and honest way using the skills of trustworthiness, political astuteness, self-confidence and personal drive. This might be seen as the capability to manage inter-personal relationships.

- Managing your feelings so that they are expressed appropriately and effectively and so achieving a desired goal. In this sense you have the capability to manage your intra-personal emotions within yourself.

We can acquire or buy this emotional currency in many different ways. For the inter-personal capability we might attend a course to develop our capability to listen, ask for feedback at the end of an interview session or receive coaching support from a senior manager. If we want to learn more about our intra-personal capabilities then we might choose to spend more time reflecting on our ability to achieve desired goals, ask for feedback from friends on certain emotional traits, or simply keep a diary to track how we manage life's ups and downs. At the end of the day all of these acts incur a cost. This might be a financial transaction as we pay to attend a course. It may be the time cost as we have to diary out time to be away from the family for a while. Finally, it might be a political or emotional trade as we put ourselves in an awkward situation when we ask for feedback from colleagues. The assertion is that in the same way we have to trade for anything in life, there will always be a cost (however imperceptible) to the acquisition of new knowledge.

" There will always be a cost (however imperceptible) to the acquisition of new knowledge "

The sell side of the heart currency can be seen in the way we are able to form relationships with colleagues and customers. This is often known as customer capital, where the relationship of a company to its customers is distinct from that of its dealings with employees and strategic partners. This relationship is of central importance to the company's worth.[10] This is where the cash flow starts, as it is in the relationship with the customers that personal capital turns into money.[11]

I worked with one project team that comprised specialists in a highly political and profitable area who were recognized as leading experts within the field. An outsider might assume that their primary focus and currency with the environment was at a head level, where people would be trading information and ideas with them. However, after deconstructing their knowledge framework against the K-Profile, it turned out that their core currency was at a heart level. Because they were effectively information brokers, operating in a buoyant and competitive market, their ability to trade information rested on their capacity to build close and effective relationship with peers, customers and competitors.

When we consider all three areas, it becomes possible to understand how we use the idea of head, hands and heart currencies to trade with the world. These can be seen in the example of simple buy and sell functions for each currency in Fig. 5.1.

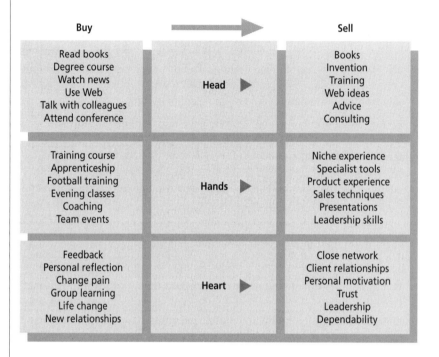

Buy	Head ▶	Sell
Read books Degree course Watch news Use Web Talk with colleagues Attend conference		Books Invention Training Web ideas Advice Consulting
Training course Apprenticeship Football training Evening classes Coaching Team events	Hands ▶	Niche experience Specialist tools Product experience Sales techniques Presentations Leadership skills
Feedback Personal reflection Change pain Group learning Life change New relationships	Heart ▶	Close network Client relationships Personal motivation Trust Leadership Dependability

Figure 5.1

Tom Peters cites a quote by Robert Louis Stevenson that 'everyone lives by selling something'.[12] The idea behind this part of the K-Profile is to help people to understand how they acquire the capability in the first place. The next stage is to understand what happens between these two stages – how does the knowledge flow from the buy to sell position and what decisions are taken on the way?

Knowledge flow

The creation of personal capital is based upon our capacity to discover new knowledge, where necessary add value and then deliver it to the market at a competitive rate. Knowledge is capital and capital can be looked at in terms of stocks and flows. At any moment in time there is a stock of knowledge; during any period of time there is a flow of knowledge.[13] Hence we can consider five core elements that might be seen within an individual's knowledge stock and flow framework.

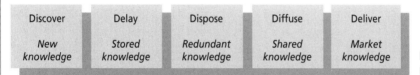

Discover	Delay	Dispose	Diffuse	Deliver
New knowledge	Stored knowledge	Redundant knowledge	Shared knowledge	Market knowledge

Figure 5.2
Flow choices

The five operations or choices are based around the idea that, when processed, knowledge will go through any one of five stages. It is important to note that this model is not offered as a de-facto standard. Rather it is intended to be a symbolic model that will help you to conceptualize what is an extremely complex series of actions. The five flow stages are:

- discover – the acquisition of new knowledge;
- delay – the storage of knowledge that is not being delivered to market;
- dispose – the process of letting go or unlearning;
- diffuse – the ability to enhance the value of knowledge through sharing;
- deliver – creating a market value by selling the knowledge.

The important thing about the flow process is that it makes conscious what is often an unconscious process. So often people will treat each stage in isolation without considering the whole picture. The degree student will focus on acquiring new knowledge but not consider how he or she might generate market value at the end of the acquisition process; an individual might start to use a personal log book to store important ideas, but fail to consider that only the explicit facts are being recorded and thus lose the tacit elements; or the team manager might spend days at a team work-shop trying to enhance the sharing process, but fail to understand how all the shared knowledge can be used to create market value.

Each of the five stages of the flow model is considered in more depth in the following chapters. At the start of each chapter, the stock and currency elements are drawn together to show how they act within that particular stage of the flow model, as seen in Fig. 5.3.

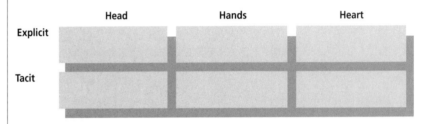

Figure 5.3
Flow matrix

This matrix is the first stage of the build towards the complete K-Profile. So when you consider the first stage of discovery, the matrix will help you think in more depth about your learning processes. At the explicit level, consider how you acquire new ideas and thoughts; or how you acquire new skills or emotional capabilities. At the tacit level, you might start to consider how you acquire new intuitive ideas, behaviours or emotions. This approach is taken through all five stages of the flow model, such that by the end you will have started to think in real depth about how you dis-cover, delay, dispose, diffuse and deliver your personal capital to market.

6

Knowledge discovery

The desire of knowledge, like the thirst of riches,
increases ever with the acquisition of it.

Laurence Sterne

Discovery is the process by which we enhance the quantity and quality of our knowledge stock. This might be through a range of processes, including reading, writing, conference presentations, working alongside someone, daydreaming, or working in a management team. The one thing they all have in common is the acquisition of knowledge using both known and unknown processes. The process of knowledge acquisition and application (whether tacit or explicit) is important because it is the wellspring that creates our personal brand and market value.[1]

Acquired knowledge does not have to be newly created, only new to the individual or organization. British Petroleum gives a Thief of the Year Award to the person who has 'stolen' the best ideas in application development. The company recognizes that, when it comes to organizational knowledge, originality is less important than usefulness. Texas Instruments has created a 'Not Invented Here, but I Did It Anyway' award for borrowing a practice from either inside or outside the company. The knowledge-focused firm needs to have appropriate knowledge available when and where it can be applied, not just generate new ideas for their own sake.

The most direct, and often most effective, way for an organization to acquire knowledge is to buy it, that is, to buy an organization or hire individuals who have a specific capability. Increasingly, companies acquire other companies specifically for their knowledge. They are often willing to pay a premium over the market value of the company because of the value they expect to get from adding that new knowledge to their own knowledge stock. One example of this was IBM's 1995 purchase of Lotus. IBM paid $3.5 billion, which was 14 times Lotus' book valuation of $250 million. Clearly, IBM did not pay that amount of money for the revenue generated by Notes and other Lotus products or for Lotus' manufacturing and sales capabilities. The $3.25 billion premium IBM paid represents its appraisal of Lotus' unique knowledge of Notes and other collaborative software applications. The minds that invented Notes are more valuable than the software itself.[2]

Discover matrix

	Head	Hand	Heart
Explicit	Acquire mental models through a codified process	Acquire skills through a codified process	Acquire emotional capabilities through a codified process
Tacit	Acquire mental models through intuition or association	Acquire new skills by intuition or association	Acquire emotional capabilities by intuition or association

Figure 6.1
Discover knowledge matrix

The discovery process will draw upon one or more of the knowledge components shown in the matrix in Fig. 6.1.

Explicit head

This is one of the more common forms of knowledge acquisition. The page you are reading now, the news you watched on television last night, or the conversation with your friend last Saturday night are all forms of explicit head discovery. Essentially, you are accepting a new mental model or schema and consciously assimilating or accommodating it into your world map.

Explicit hand

Again, this is a common process by which knowledge is acquired. One of the most common ways to do this is to attend a course, learn to play a guitar, or to type at 80 words per minute.

Explicit heart

This is how you enhance your emotional understanding of a situation. This might be an interpersonal capability, whereby you engage your ability to manage a difficult relationship or coach a colleague through a problem. Alternatively, it might be an intrapersonal growth, where you develop a greater understanding about your self-motivation or capability to change yourself.

Tacit head

The discovery of tacit cognitive knowledge is something that will happen subtly and possibly over a longer period. This is because the tacit capability is hard to verbalize because it is expressed through action and cannot be reduced to specific rules and operations. So the discovery of tacit head knowledge might be seen in the way you will gently grow your understanding about the norms and culture within an organization. Think about how you acquired your beliefs, perceptions and mental models. They are possibly so ingrained that you don't even know what they are.

Tacit hand

This is the absorption or internalization of skills and behaviours at a deep and often unknowing level. This is a process where the acquisition of knowledge is made through the example of others. Thus apprentices learn their craft by following and copying their masters; doctors learn skills through periods of internship; and new employees are immersed in on-the-job training with existing team members.

● Tacit heart

This is how we acquire new emotional understanding about others or ourselves. Again, this is something that generally happens through association and close relationships. The acquisition of tacit heart knowledge is often something that we do unconsciously every minute of the day. Our feelings that change as we get close to a working colleague; the values we form when joining a new team; or the shift in emotions we form about a new product are all examples of the discovery of tacit heart knowledge. Emotion provides the primary feedback mechanism, that alerts the person that various goals are not being achieved and this in turn motivates behaviour. Emotion arouses the dissatisfaction with the current state of affairs when a person compares the newly perceived reality unfavourably with his or her prior expectations. This often stimulates the learning and knowledge discovery process.[3]

Although the knowledge components are separated in the matrix, this is not to suggest that they operate independently. Clearly, the acquisition of explicit head knowledge is dependent upon your explicit and tacit feelings about a person, product or context. In the same way, the acquisition of tacit behavioural knowledge will be affected by the explicit beliefs that you have along with the existing skill set.

When we look at the discover process, the whole process is driven by personal beliefs, experience and preferences, so it is impossible to consider in depth how differently we actually acquire knowledge. There are three important questions that we should ask in relation to the process of knowledge discovery.

● What filters do I use that enhance or block my ability to acquire knowledge?

● How do I create new knowledge?

● What investment strategies do I employ that ensure I acquire value added knowledge?

By asking these three questions, you are starting down the road of making conscious what is so often an unconscious process.

Discover filters

Before you can start to understand your discovery processes, you need to appreciate how you make sense of the world. Think about the last time you went to see a film with a friend or partner. It is amazing how, at the end, two people can share the same experience but emerge with such differing views on the content and style of the film. Whereas you might focus on the story, your friend might come out having seen the political metaphors that are used to underpin the storyline. So, although you have experienced that same activity, the filters used to make sense of the world have modified your perception.

The basis of these filters is that because the brain has so much information to process, it tries to make sense of the world by putting incoming data into familiar shapes and forms. These shapes allow us make sense of the information as it enters our body and more importantly place value on the content.

Although there are many perceptual filters, some of the more common ones are described below.

Time filter

We often filter around three different points in time: the future, the past or the present. Consider the company director. If 'past-based', he or she will refer to the successes and the deep-rooted values that helped the company to survive. The future-orientated director will talk about the five-year plan, the next acquisition or expansion into new markets. The present-based director might focus on the here and now, will not be interested in past successes and will have little desire to discuss long-term plans.

Information filter

Another filtration process is seen in the way that we 'chunk' information. One person may take a conceptual view of the world, looking at global markets, total system changes or the entire customer base. Another considers the small detail in a proposal. They might leave the large chunks of information to the specialists but need to understand specific details in a situation.

● Direction filters

Some of us view change and disruption as a problem, seeing life as an obstacle course that has to be tackled every day. Others see life as a basket of opportunities, a rich world that throws up chances for people to grow and develop. The former will see a situation as an opportunity and talk about 'walking towards' it. The problem-centred person might view it as a negative issue, something he or she is trying to 'move away' from.

● Referencing filter

This is the way that someone might measure success. Are they externally referenced, such that they feel that the customer service results, market share or stock price indicates the level of success? Or are they internally referenced, with their focus on internal measures, feeling good when morale surveys or process measures indicate they are performing well?

● Association filter

Some people might talk about a problem in terms that indicate their personal pain or concerns about how it impacts on a situation. Another will take a distanced view, talking about the issue as an objective commentator, not positioning it as something in which he or she is personally involved.

" To understand your filters, you need to be able to take a cold and dispassionate look at yourself from outside in "

These filters are immensely important to the discover process. Although they can speed up our ability to absorb and process information, they can also limit our capability to stretch and move beyond the current frame of reference. As such it is important that you take time out to map and understand your personal filters and how they restrict the acquisition process.

To understand your filters, you need to be able to take a cold and dispassionate look at yourself from outside in. Think about the last time you acquired a new piece of knowledge and then relate it to the filters. Did you select it because it will help you in the future, or is it related to what is happening now? Might it be seen as a large chunk of knowledge, i.e. concerned with grand ideas, or a small chunk in that it was quite detailed. By analyzing your knowledge acquisition processes you can start to understand not only the knowledge that you filter in but, more importantly, the knowledge that you might subconsciously filter out. It might be that your filters act as a block to prevent you from acquiring knowledge that has higher market value than that which you currently discover. If so, you need to ensure that compensating strategies are employed to remove the blockade and so open up the incoming knowledge channels.

Digging for gold

Although it is impossible to outline all the processes that we use to gather new knowledge, there are a number of fundamental ones that we should all be practising on a regular basis. As you read through each of the following five examples, ask yourself some questions. Consider how often you practise this activity, how well you manage it and what approach offers you the best opportunity to gather knowledge that will be of value to the market.

Intuition

In a recent study, eighty-two of the ninety-three winners of the Nobel Peace Prize over a sixteen-year period agreed that intuition plays an important part in creative and scientific discoveries.[4] This suggests that what might normally be perceived as a structured scientific approach to life (hypotheses, forecast, experiment and analysis), is actually improved through the use of the softer or emotionally-based factors.

Intuition is driven by human emotion rather than any logical cause-effect analysis. It is the ability of the individual to have a hunch that something might work or the ability to see with the heart.[5] There are three key components that can contribute towards developing an enhanced sense of practical intuition:

- **Attentiveness** – placing an increased emphasis on the inner voice and the gut feelings that we have but often ignore.
- **Questioning** – placing greater importance on the idea of asking others what they mean, what they see and what they feel about things.
- **Curiosity** – extending the ability to become interested in the boring and excited about the mundane.

You can choose to influence your ability to take intuitive decisions. For example, when in a meeting, you have the choice to frame your mind-set for each of these three factors. To sit and actively listen and really internalize the points that are being made rather than being outside the flow that takes place in the meeting (increased attentiveness). By using questions that are focused on our feelings, ideas, thoughts and beliefs, the breadth and depth of enquiry can be enhanced (questioning). Finally, by looking at people's body language, listening to the words they use and being closely aware of the environment, you might become excited by the surroundings (curiosity).

However, it is important to emphasize that the special focus on intuition does not mean that it precludes the notion of rationality. Although intuitive insights can appear not to make sense and might seem to be the opposite of a rational response, when brought together they actually form a more powerful way in which to create new ideas. Einstein never discovered anything with his rational mind – the principle of relativity came about after he had a dream where he saw himself travelling on a beam of light. This intuitive idea, coupled with his brilliance as a physicist, allowed him to develop a scientific theory that helped change the world's view of itself.

Experience

One of the primary sources of commercial knowledge is the personal experiences that we have every day. Buyers for supermarkets do not live that role for 24 hours a day. They might also be a parent who experiences the products on a personal as well as a professional level. This is just a simple example of the life experiences that an individual will bring to the workplace. The question is, to what extent are you able to draw upon the fountain of knowledge and skills?

If you are serious about learning and creating knowledge, consider the extent to which you consciously milk personal experiences. You have a rich diversity that might not be fully utilized in that you have a home life, handicaps, hobbies and holidays. Wherever possible draw upon this as a tool to generate new ideas and skills in the workplace.

Scanning

The discovery of knowledge that is totally new is often impractical and unrealistic. The market is ever changing and fickle and, therefore as such, you need to constantly monitor new trends, products and services as they emerge. This offers the idea of active borrowing, scanning or searching the external world for ideas and inspiration.

Although the way in which this is undertaken will vary, there are a number of common approaches that can be identified. These are built around two key variables. First is the breadth of the search – is the exploration based within the same industry grouping or does it move into an industry that is totally different? The second variable is the balance between a passive and active search. For a passive search, you might put search systems in place and wait for new ideas to surface. Alternatively, do you actively go out to search for new ideas in a proactive way? The relationship between these two continuums produces the matrix shown below.

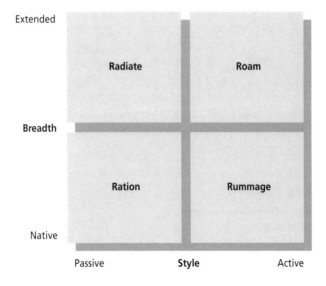

Figure 6.2

- **Ration.** In this case, you only have a limited interest in searching outside your domain for new ideas. The passive approach might be to subscribe to industry journals or join committees to help develop industry specifications and standards. Although the discovery process is enabled, it is unlikely to provide any real stretch or diversity in the way you think or the knowledge you acquire.

- **Radiate.** Here, you recognize that ideas from other areas might be of interest but little positive action is taken to pick up on them. Examples might be subscribing to journals from other industries, attending trade shows, or attending conferences in different fields.

- **Rummage.** In this case you take the time to interact closely with other people from the same industry in order to identify new opportunities. When attending conferences you might present best practice from your area and invite people to work on joint developments. In this way, the discovery process is focused on depth and developing specific expertise in a niche area.

- **Roam.** For this quadrant you have taken a positive decision to look aggressively for inspiration beyond the local domain. It might be that you look for a counterpart in other companies and initiate a process of dialogue with them. One example might be supporting personal development by attending cross-industry management programmes. Practices such as job swaps or sabbaticals might also help develop your capacity to think in a divergent way. The goal is to suck in knowledge that is both diverse in form and rigorous in depth, to form a broad spread of opportunities.

Whatever the style, you need to consider how effective your scanning processes are. For example, do you have the freedom to do independent roams, or do you need to obtain permission from the business before you look outside the organization for new ideas? Are you allowed to set up cross-industry relationships without worrying about the chance that some of the company's secrets might be released? No one style is right. The important thing is for you to recognize the benefits that are accrued from the scanning process and not just to assume that innovation will only come from the area where you currently operate.

Serendipity

In simple terms, this might be defined as the gift for making a fortunate discovery accidentally. Stories abound of the various inventions that have emerged from the process of serendipity: Goodyear's accidental discovery of the vulcanization process for rubber, or Fleming's accidental discovery of penicillin. All of these originated because someone (apparently) happened to be in the right place at the right time and was observant enough to notice something out of the ordinary.

However, simply being around when an accident happens is not enough to bring about new ideas and discoveries. The key is to be in a state of constant preparedness and to recognize the difference between an accident and when fate has offered the chance to create something new. So a discovery based on serendipity might be seen as the fruit of a seed sown by chance in fertile ground.[6]

The idea of 'fertile ground' is an engaging one and merits further discussion. How can you create the fertile ground to allow for discovery based on serendipity? The most important factor is to be in a constant state of readiness. All of the ideas discussed so far in the book contribute directly to your capability and willingness to search for fortunate accidents. In essence, to develop a personal style where you are enabled, energized and ready to snatch opportunities as they surface.

Relationships

Learning as a result of interaction with other people is a key component in the knowledge creation process. There are times when something exciting happens between two people, a materialization that would not have happened to an individual. This relational discovery process can take place in two forms, either at the tacit or explicit level. Tacit relational discovery might occur where you work with someone else for a period of time but do not recognize any improvement in your working method. Alternatively, relational discovery can take place at the explicit level, for example, the surprises that can emerge as a team goes through a problem-solving process together. The dynamic interaction that takes place between tacit, explicit and relational knowledge creates the flow of energy that is necessary to stimulate the discovery of new ideas.

The relational factor is of great importance with respect to the idea of serendipity. It is very rare that one could explicitly point to an idea that one person solely originated without help (known or unknown) from another human being. We are all subject to influence in our creative process, be it positively or negatively. The development of new ideas can be a buoyant process in which your random thoughts might trigger an idea in another, which in turn leads to a prototype by someone else. Hence, it is the social construction of knowledge that is potentially most valuable in creating personal capital.

Discover strategy

When we try to create or discover new knowledge, it is easy to waste our personal time and energy. We can spend hours, days and even months working on a project or attending a course, only to realize that its actual market value is limited. Think of the last time you attended a training course. Although you might have looked at the objectives and considered how they might help you to perform your job, did you really undertake a time/value analysis to consider how the acquired knowledge (rather than the certificate) would grow your personal worth? Even more, did you map this against the time you would invest and how this time might be better spent elsewhere?

There are two key questions that need to be considered about the discovery process.

- How much time should I allocate to the discovery stage?
- How much value will the discovery yield?

Your answers to these questions should readily map onto the matrix shown in Fig. 6.3.

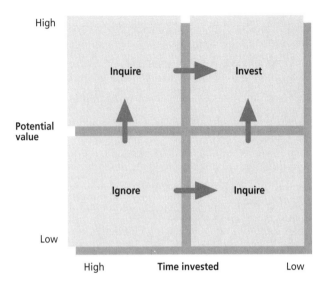

Figure 6.3
Discover strategy

Ignore

If your response sits in this box then don't even think about it. I have seen so many people go into the discovery process without the faintest clue as to why they are spending time on the activity and without any idea of how it will enhance their market value. Just look at your diary for the next three months – there is probably an entry in there that says 'attend conference', 'go to workshop' or 'attend a training course'. Now ask yourself: How much real value will I be able to create in the market as a result of spending this time? If you don't know, then it behoves you to either find out, or find a better way to spend that time.

Inquire

The inquire box is the marginal activity. It is the time you spend where the payback might not warrant the initial investment. For the high value/high time quadrant – clearly it is necessary to generate a high value knowledge return, but the question must always be: 'Could I have achieved this value without spending so much time?' If you are about to invest three days of your time to learn a new management technique, question whether you need to go on a course to learn it, or do you have the capability to gain the information from a book. This way the time/value ratio is maximized, such that you can spend time on other value enhancing activities. The alternative is the low value/low time quadrant. Although the time is only limited, you still might question whether there are alternative activities that you could undertake to generate increased value. Alternatively, could you change the outcome so that it would become a high value gain?

Invest

Finally, any response in this matrix is almost certainly something worth investment in. If you can spend minimal time on an activity that will enhance your personal value, then unless there are hidden downsides, time should be allocated.

Although this is a simple model, the idea is more about the thought processes that drive the decision making than the model itself. For example, you might be about to go on a course that has been poorly received by colleagues. The assumption is that this would sit in the ignore quadrant, but you have the choice to reframe the time investment. If the course will include people who you would like to meet or network with, then you can start to reconsider what value you might derive. It might be that the value you derive is not the value that the course designer envisaged, but that is OK. The important thing is always to question the time/value relationship. If there is no clear personal gain for you in investing time, then you should question the point of doing so.

For example, I regularly try to go on courses even if I don't believe that the content will be of any real value to me or my business. As a consultant, part of my delivery value is the ability to build effective relationships with other people in a learning environment. Now, one of the problems that trainers can face is to disconnect from the role of delegate. If I spend all my time delivering courses, I forget what it feels like to be in a room to learn from someone else. This can create a sense of arrogance and unprofessionalism in the way that I present my programmes. By attending courses, I get to re-discover what it feels like to be a delegate, sometimes a delegate in a situation I don't really want to be in. For me, this creates real value in the explicit and tacit heart parts of the K-Profile.

One example of the way that companies are investing in the discovery process can be seen in the way that the learning process itself is being enhanced. Many companies now offer a flat figure of several hundreds of pounds for employees to undertake a course of their choice. This can be sewing, horse riding, playing the bongos or even skydiving. The more astute organizations have realized that investing in the process of learning can be as big a reward as growing the content of people's knowledge base. Interestingly, people are often critical of this process because it is seen as investing in areas that will not add value to the business. The trick is to understand that knowledge discovery is a rich and complex process and as such we need to be very clear as to what is being gained and what ultimately the end value will be.

"Investing in the process of learning can be as big a reward as growing the content of people's knowledge base"

Remember, you have choice about where you sit in the matrix. If you find that much of your discovery time is spent in the ignore or inquire quadrant, then ask yourself why. It might be because colleagues, peers or partners are pressuring you, or it might be that you get to sessions only to find that they offer little value. The reality is that you have to take action to get into the invest quadrant because no one else will. The good news is that this quadrant is like a muscle: It will grow and expand as you spend more time working in it. As you become effective in acquiring high-value knowledge, so your peers will recognize a growth in your personal value and will aspire to spend more time in your company. The end result is that you get to choose whom you want to spend time with and how much value can be derived from the time.

To reiterate, when the models ask about the payback in terms of value, this is not necessarily a financial return. This is about a reward that fits in with your personal goals. If your aim is to grow value by helping others or giving blood, then the payback is the satisfaction of doing that and doing it to the best of your ability. Altruism is an important part of the framework and it must never be overlooked. The idea of payback in feelings rather than kind was illustrated by a story about blood donation. In Britain, blood is given free of charge. Donors are proud to be known as good, altruistic people. There is rarely a shortage and, importantly, the quality of blood is very high because the healthiest people give blood. In America, it's the opposite. People are frequently paid to give blood and so you've got two big problems: the quality of blood is bad, because drug addicts and the poor have an incentive to donate, and there tend to be many shortages of blood.

A couple of years ago, there was talk in Britain about selling blood to make money for the new blood-donor service. Immediately there was an uproar. People didn't want to give blood, even though that money was to go back into the blood-donor service. People felt it was no longer a gift relationship. The number of people giving blood dropped dramatically in the weeks following that decision. The currency changed! Therefore, the emotions changed. When someone gives you money, you don't feel the same emotions that you feel when someone demonstrates a kindness. We are too quick to interpret everything as marginal that does not fit our economic model. The risk is that when one person tries to equate his or her currency value against that valued by someone else confusion can arise.[7]

Finally, the idea of knowledge discovery can be viewed at many levels. If it makes sense for an individual to manage the knowledge discovery process, then it also makes sense for a team or company to follow the same ground rules. Consider how many companies spend time on developing new strategies but fail to consider what knowledge will be necessary to deliver the end strategy. Just consider the fashion business, the whole basis of a company's survival will depend upon the capability to forecast what will be in fashion and to then deliver against this projected knowledge. So consider the trouser manufacturer that decides that flares will be the next big thing. They make the decision to launch a distinctive bell-bottom product. If the strategy works, one million consumers would forgo straight leg trousers when they next buy a pair of jeans and instead go for the flared look. The fashion business is ruthlessly competitive. Winning depends on predictive knowledge. The development of the new flared trousers will be the culmination of an elaborate knowledge process of development and testing by designers, buyers and production engineers. Part science, part art and a little bit of luck, the new style is crafted by a team of industrial knowledge workers – men and women applying their special skills, their accumulated experience and knowledge of fashion to the challenge of inventing the next one million-seller hit. This is the discovery process acquiring knowledge that will have end value, not knowledge for the sake of it.

The capability to discover new knowledge is now a real business issue. After spending most of the last two decades trying to slash their way to profitability, most companies have come to realize that a corporate strategy of self-mutilation is not the path to longevity. Nor, for that matter, is it a pure technology play, since there's virtually nothing you can invent, license or buy that your rivals can't match. The only real potential for future growth is in your head, heart and hands. Smart companies now realize they must innovate their way to profitability and after that, they have to keep on innovating.[8] If that is true, then we need to help individuals learn how to innovate and derive personal and business value from the innovation.

> *"The capability to discover new knowledge is now a real business issue"*

Discover questions

- Can you describe the top five ways that you discover knowledge?

- How would your friends or colleagues rate your ability to create and acquire new knowledge?

- Is your preference to acquire knowledge through the explicit or tacit channel?

- Which do you prefer to acquire head, hand or heart knowledge and why?

- Of these three, which do you least prefer to acquire?

- What filters do you use to make sense of the world?

- When you discover new things about working with people, how do you translate them into market value?

- What was your last creative act and how did you manage it?

- How much do you use intuition to create knowledge? How effective is it for you, i.e. does it deliver an end-market value?

- Name three people with whom you recently created or discovered knowledge?

- What is your preferred process for scanning the market to discover new types of knowledge?

- How much time do you spend on knowledge discovery?

- How much time should you spend on knowledge discovery?

- List the people you know who are best at discovering new knowledge – what is it that they do that makes them so effective?

7

Knowledge delay

Any piece of knowledge I acquire today has a value at this moment exactly proportional to my skill to deal with it. Tomorrow, when I know more, I recall that piece of knowledge and use it better.

Mark Van Doren

The storage process aligns with each of the currencies (head, hand and heart). Head storage is knowledge held within our mental models. Behavioural knowledge is stored within the muscle and retains the ability to perform a particular act. Heart storage is the unconscious and conscious feelings stored in the amygdala in the brain. This is the part of the brain that retains the emotional flavour that goes with facts about a certain situation or act. An individual's ability to manage all three areas will offer the chance to draw upon a stock of knowledge whenever convenient.

So if discovery, diffusion and delivery are about flow, then this aspect is the stock area, where knowledge is temporarily or permanently stored ready for retrieval at a later time. This might be a ten second delay, as you think over a new idea to put to a project team, or a one year delay as you store a management report on your hard disk.

There are two key points to consider with this stage: (1) Do you understand how you manage the storage process? and (2) What is your capability to retrieve stored knowledge on demand? Often we take a casual or even sloppy approach to this stage of the model. For this reason, vast chunks of potential personal value are wasted either because we don't actually record or lock in new ideas or thoughts as they come into our worldview or because we are unable to recall or access stored information when it can be used in the market.

If you want to think about your delay processes stop reading the book now and get yourself a pen and paper.

Just take a few minutes to reflect on what has happened since you started to read this book. Note down the process you followed and how you have sorted the information offered thus far. Have you taken notes?; have you assumed that any useful ideas will be stored in your memory?; have you made notes on any of the pages where you found something of interest?; or have you coded ideas into a logbook? There is no right way to manage your storage process, but it is important that you understand how you manage it. Otherwise all of the information and knowledge that enters the discovery stage every day can be lost or frittered away because of poor or limited storage strategies.

Delay matrix

	Head	Hand	Heart
Explicit	Store known ideas for retrieval later	Store codified skills for retrieval later	Store known emotions for retrieval later
Tacit	Store intuitive ideas for retrieval later	Store intuitive skills for retrieval later	Store intuitive emotions for retrieval later

Figure 7.1

Explicit head

These are the ideas, rules and models that we use to drive our decision-making processes. This might be the process we have to follow when making a company presentation or the structure of the financial report when submitted to the project control board.

Explicit hand

This is the skill that we have stored away to enact a particular function or performance. Examples might be the ability to play a guitar, accurately pass a ball on a football pitch, or train a group of unruly teenagers in a classroom. These are physical capabilities that you are able to readily display to another person.

Explicit heart

These are the personal strategies and styles that you use to manage your emotional life and relationship with others. This might be the way that you communicate the vision of the company, how you plan to undergo negotiations with a difficult customer, or the visualization process you follow to prepare yourself in advance of an important presentation. The primary test is that you are able to describe the emotions you are using and how they are being applied.

Tacit head

These are the subtle and intuitive models and structures used to manage your life. This might be how you would avoid certain areas of the town because you feel they are dangerous, the mental maps that help you to decide if a new customer is likely to be a good credit risk, or the deep set patterns that a master chess player is able to automatically recognize. The critical point is that someone else might be able to recognize that you are using a certain way of thinking, but you might find it difficult to lucidly describe the mental model you are using or how it is being applied.

Tacit hand

This is the unconscious, learnt behaviour that we use to perform particular activities. This might be the way that a champion swimmer is able to glide through the water, the lead guitarist is able to play at speed but with finesse and the team leader manages to lead a particularly difficult quality group meeting. Again, as with the tacit head elements, others will probably see the capability in you before you see it in yourself. Consider the ballerina who creates a market value from her ability to learn and store a range of complex motor patterns. It is unlikely that she will be able to describe each step she takes and how she performs the move, as the skills are learnt through a disciplined and lengthy training programme starting from a young age.

Tacit heart

These stored emotions are the ones we use to make deep-seated personal judgements and build effective relationships. This can be seen in the way we diffuse arguments between friends, build networks to support a new project office, or overcome personal adversity and barriers. One of the most simple but powerful tacit emotional tools that we use is the capability to build trust with others. You will be able to think of people now who have an amazing capacity to create high trust relationships wherever they go – and I am sure that you can think of others who operate in a world of deceit and duplicity.

The idea of knowledge delay or storage can be a difficult one to deal with. Although it is something that we do from birth, it isn't often that we are encouraged to sit back and reflect on just how we hold onto and manage this stock of personal capital. In the following sections I offer a number of ideas that might help you to move down this road and think about how you can effectively manage your ability to store and retrieve knowledge on demand. The key questions are as follows.

● How effective is my memory as a storage system?

● How do I use systems to retain information?

● What impact do emotions have on my storage capability?

● Do I store knowledge in partnership with other people?

These questions might seem relativity easy to answer, but in reality they underpin your entire capacity to create a market value. Consider any management meeting that you have recently attended. The session was probably full of ideas, questions, challenges and emotional learning. Now think about how much of that knowledge was actually taken away and translated into something with real market value. In my experience up to 90% of all 'potential' knowledge created in a team or organization is lost because of poor or missing processes to capture and harness the knowledge. Unless we ask these types of questions and make the delay process explicit then we are not capturing capital for future exploitation.

Fluid, fixed or firm

The purpose of this stage in the model is to consider how we store, retain and reuse knowledge that has been stockpiled for later use. The matrix considers primarily the human or fluid aspect of storage, there is also the issue of fixed storage – i.e. logging information on paper, in a system or even on a clay tablet.

The delay process can be considered in three ways: Fluid; Fixed and Firm. Although this offers a slightly simplistic view of the asset categories, it does help to understand how we structure and manage our knowledge.

Fluid

These are elements of knowledge that are contained within our hearts and minds and leave when we leave the business. It might be personal experience accumulated over a number of years in the business, or a long-term relationship cultivated with a customer. Sometimes it can be shared knowledge that has yet to be coded into the organization's systems and processes. This might be an idea that a person has submitted, but that has been excluded or lost in the internal system. The bottom line is that if the person leaves, so does the knowledge.

Fixed

These are knowledge elements retained when an individual leaves. Once knowledge is locked in the system as coded information, it can be seen as hard capital. It is available for anyone in the company to make use of it, irrespective of the originator's presence. Such examples might be coded software, product upgrades or business proposals.

Firm

This is knowledge that sits between the fixed and fluid model in that it has a dependency on both elements. This might be the unique sound that is produced from a musical genius playing a quality instrument. Individually each of the elements can perform to a satisfactory degree, but in bringing the two together, there is an added presence, a synergy that enhances the levels of knowledge. The knowledge might only be available when two separate elements are brought together, like the need for two opposing polarities to generate an electrical current. An example might be where an individual has independently created a database. Anyone else who attempts to use it will not be able to extract the information, because they do not have an intimate appreciation of the system's architecture.

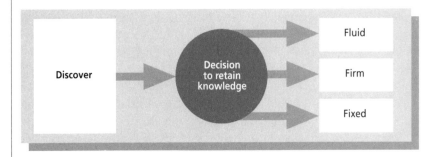

Figure 7.2

● Fluid delay

Memory has often been compared to a storehouse. This conception goes back to Greek philosophers and to St Augustine, who described the 'roomy chambers of memory where are the treasures of countless images ...' This special metaphor, which likens memories to objects that are put into storage compartments, held for a while, then searched for is a recurrent theme in both ancient and modern thought. It is this simple but powerful image that has been used to build the symbolic model that represents the fluid aspects of storage within the delay phase of the model.

The word memory has a variety of meanings and has been defined in many ways. The purpose in this section of the book is not to provide the answer to how we remember, but to offer a simple framework that might help you to manage knowledge to be used at a later date.

I believe that we need to develop personal systems to manage our storage processes because so much of what we learn is lost in the stream of information that we acquire. As the philosopher, William James said in 1890, 'the stream of thought flows on, but most of its elements fall into the bottomless pit of oblivion. Of some, no element survives the instant of their passage. Of others, it is confined to a few moments, hours or days. Others again, leave vestiges which are indestructible and by means of which they may be recalled for as long as possible.'[1] So often we acquire an idea, think of a new way to resolve a problem or meet a contact, but the moment is lost when another thought enters our head.

To understand how we manage the storage process we must first understand the simple dynamics of human memory. The view offered in this section of the book is not meant to be a definitive explanation of the various head, hand and heart processes by which human beings codify and store information. The object is to offer a simple but effective model that will help to make sense of the storage process. This is built around the assumption that our memory consists of three different areas: sensory, short-term and long-term.

Sensory memory

The world is full of information that we have to acquire and manage on a second by second basis. The first component of the memory system that has to deal with external information are the sensory registers. These receive large amounts of information from all the senses (visual, auditory, touch, smell and taste).

The first function of the sensory memory is to retain information for a period of time long enough to enable us to decide if the information has value and should be stored for a longer period. The encoding of information in the sensory memory is related to the process of transduction. This is the transformation of sensory information from the environment into the neural impulses that can be processed by our sensory system and the brain. For example, if we look at the sensory process within the eye, an image applied to the retina lasts for a few tenths of a second after the image has gone. So if you watch someone wave a lighted cigarette in a dark room, a streak rather than a series of points will be seen, indicating the persistence of the image when the stimulus has disappeared. Since humans have several sensory channels to market, it is likely that sensory memory exists for each, although much of the research has been on the visual and auditory memory.[2]

The importance of sensory memory to the knowledge process cannot be underestimated. First, we must learn to pay attention to information if we are to manage its absorption. Second, it takes time to bring all the sensory information into the consciousness, so this process must be managed. For example, if you are bombarded with an overload of external data then you will have difficulty in absorbing any of it. Even worse, within that onslaught there are bound to be pearls of wisdoms that could enhance your personal market value.

Short-term (working) memory

Once the information leaves the sensory memory, it can either be discarded or transferred to the short-term or working memory. This is the storage system that can hold a limited amount of information for a few seconds. It is the part of the memory where information that is currently being thought about can be stored. Hence, the thoughts we are having at any moment in time are being processed in this working memory and when we start to think about the topic it will either be lost or transferred to the long-term storage system. Hence, the most important thing about the short-term memory is not its duration, but the fact that it is active. This is the area where knowledge is operated on, organized for storage, connected to other information, or discarded.

" Short-term memory has been shown to be anything between three and eighteen seconds"

Remember the number 783445. Now close your eyes and repeat it and then count backwards from 99 to 91 by 2s and try repeating the number again. The chances are that you can't.[3] This is because you are trying to process two separate tasks in the same, shared working space, an area that is referred to as the short-term memory. Although you started out using

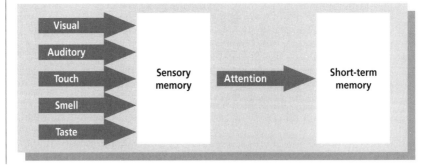

Figure 7.3
Sensory and short-term memory

the space to store the six-digit number, once you had to process a separate set of numbers they effectively knocked the initial set out of the working space. This workspace is an area where current knowledge processing and storage takes place, something akin to the random access memory (RAM) on your personal computer. In the same way this workspace is utilized for a range of active thinking processes and several specific storage devices that are called in to play, dependent upon the function being performed.

One way to determine the capacity of short-term recall is by measuring the memory span, the number of items an individual can recall after just one presentation. For normal adults, this span is consistent. If the items are randomly chosen letters or digits, the subject can recall about seven items give or take two. This quality, seven, plus or minus two has been called the magic number. This number represents the holding capacity of our short-term memory, the number of items that will fit into the store at any one time.[4] Although this is not regarded as a specific figure and there is always some debate about its accuracy, it is a good guide when trying to manage your memory, or managing how other people learn and retain knowledge.

Short-term memory has been shown to be anything between three and eighteen seconds. The Brown Peterson technique used a process by which people were asked to recall a set of three letter codes. While people could

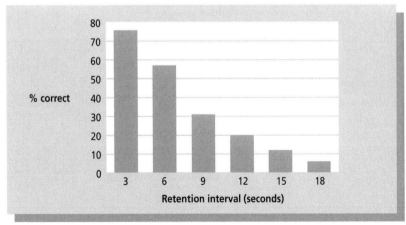

Figure 7.4
Short-term memory retention

remember the codes after a period of three seconds, after eighteen seconds this dropped to a mere 6%.

Knowledge chunking can help you to better manage your knowledge storage processes. If you try to remember forty-nine different types of car, then you are likely to fall short well before the end (unless you have a specific emotional association or experience of motor cars). However, if you first of all think of seven car manufacturers and then think of seven car types produced by each manufacturer, then there is a strong chance that your recall will be enhanced. Hence by chunking, the goal is not to try to remember all the items in a list, but to categorize them into meta-level categories.

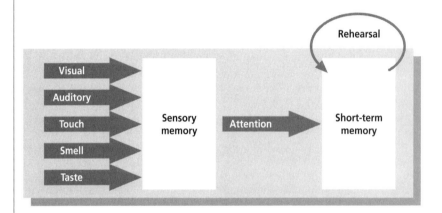

Figure 7.5
Memory rehearsal

The ability to retain ideas in the working memory is also aided by internal repetition or iteration. Think of the last time you had to remember a phone number or someone's name. The automatic response is to repeat it over and over again in your head. This is a rehearsal process and one that we use almost instinctively. Rehearsal is important because the longer an item remains in working memory, the greater the chance that it will be transferred to long-term memory. Without rehearsal, items will probably not stay in working memory for more than about 30 seconds. Because working memory also has a limited capacity, information can be lost as other information forces it out. Think again of the last time you tried to remember a number – the moment an external interruption came along (someone else talking or the phone ringing again) then it was pushed from your memory.

However, it is important to understand that rehearsal does not guarantee that the knowledge will lock into working memory for retrieval at a later date. If you are trying to remember a phone number to call the person back in ten minutes, then the rehearsal process will keep the number locked in the short-term or working memory. This is known as maintenance rehearsals, where the knowledge is learnt in a rote fashion, that is the form in which it was presented. However, once the call is made there is no guarantee that it will lock into the long-term storage. To lock knowledge into the long-term storage it is sometimes important to elaborate the information, possibly by giving it some meaning or linking it with pre-existing knowledge.

Working memory is not driven by clinical criteria and structures. The way it functions and the ways it stores knowledge will be a product of what it already knows and what prior experiences it has been through. In other words it will be driven by the content of the long-term memory. In order to understand that you are watching a game of netball, you have to understand what netball is and what it means to you personally. Only when the content of the working memory is matched with the content of the long-term memory will the two act together to form new knowledge. If the conscious processes deem this knowledge to be of value then the individual can choose to pay greater attention to the game and so discover more information about the activity. So the sensory processes will tune in to those aspects where the working memory wishes to process specific information. So, once the game of netball is recognized, the choice might be to gather data on the smell of the gym, the sounds that we make, or the kinaesthetic feel of the environment or people.

In this way, the working memory is a critical buffer in the discovery, delay, diffusion and delivery of personal knowledge. It sits at the crossroads of the knowledge flow and any mismanagement in this can lead to blockages in the inflow or outflows of knowledge. This block can in turn lead to a situation where you fail to spot valuable information in the market, or fail to deliver personal capital that is perceived by the market to be of significant value.

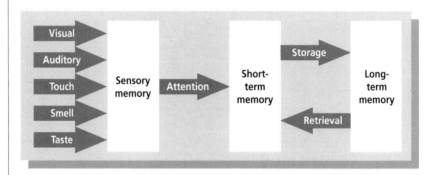

Figure 7.6

Long-term memory

Long-term memory has been conceptualized as a vast storehouse of information in which memories are stored in a relatively permanent way and it is in this storage system that information not lost from the short-term area is stored. Exactly how much information can be stored here is not known and there is no evidence of any limit to its storage capacity. So, whereas the short-term or working memory does have certain limitations, this is not so with long-term storage.

Although it is impossible to explicitly state how the long-term memory is organized, it is possible to offer a conceptual framework that highlights the structural processes used to store knowledge. There are two types of long-term memory, declarative and procedural.

Declarative memory is often known as fact memory because it is used to store the knowledge of specific elements. It might be viewed as knowledge that something has happened or knowledge of the attributes that a product might have. This type of memory can be further separated into two types of storage area, episodic and semantic memory.

Episodic memory contains the autobiographical record of people, places and events that we have encountered. One might think of it as one's own personal life movie, covering all those aspects that one would choose to remember. It is primarily about oneself and one's association with the world, for example who one went out with last night, the time one got drunk at a party, or the time one presented a management paper to the board. Answer the following question: Where is the light switch in your bedroom? In building your response you might create an image of your bedroom and then map where the switch is. In drawing upon this information you are using the episodic memory, as information is stored in the form of images that are organized on the basis of when and where events happened.

Semantic memory is the store of facts about the world, some of which are personal, but most of which form mental map that describes how the world is. This will include the concepts, rules and processes that we use to function effectively. It is stored and organized in the form of networks of ideas. As an example, most knowledge that is acquired in a classroom might fall into the semantic memory.

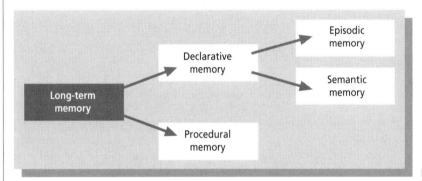

Figure 7.7

Procedural memory is referred to as the skill memory since it is held to store the knowledge of how to, for example play a guitar, kick a ball or drive a car. Unlike episodic or semantic memory, we cannot reflect upon and inspect this type of knowledge because it is concerned with the tacit or difficult skill that is hard to describe. Hence, when we learn something, we slowly encode this knowledge into a deep set of procedures that we use to function in the world. This is stored as a complex set of stimulus response pairings – so that when someone throws a ball towards us we automatically put our hands up to catch it.

Some people believe that the number of concepts or chunks of knowledge that a human expert in a particular field can master is around 50,000 to 100,000. This range appears to be valid over a wide range of human endeavours; the number of board positions mastered by a chess grand master, the concepts mastered by an expert in a technical field such as a physician, or the vocabulary of a writer (Shakespeare used 29,000 words).

These chunks of knowledge are only a small subset of the knowledge we need to function as a human being. We have to survive simply by being able to talk, read notices, converse with others and order our lunch at the canteen. The suggestion is that in total we might use something in the region of 100 million knowledge chunks or units of understanding.[5]

The goal in any storage process is to ensure that knowledge can be held safely in long-term memory and retrieved at the appropriate time. The extent to which particular knowledge chunks will be readily recalled can depend upon the processes of primacy and recency. Primacy is the suggestion that items that were first heard are likely to be more dominant in the memory system. In addition, those items that were more recently absorbed are more likely to be recalled from memory.

Emotional memory

So, once we have considered the role of memory in the delay process, what role do our emotions have on all this? Well, Daniel Goldman in his book *Emotional Intelligence* suggests that, within the first few milliseconds of our perceiving something, we not only unconsciously comprehend what it is, but decide whether we like it or not; the 'unconscious' presents our awareness with, not just identity of what we see, but an opinion about it. Our emotions have a 'mind of their own', one which can hold views quite independently of our rational mind.

Unlike conscious feelings, emotions originate in the brain at a much deeper level, using mechanisms that are only now being revealed. For example, our brains can detect danger before we even experience the feeling of being afraid. The brain also begins to initiate physical responses (heart palpitations, sweaty palms, muscle tension) before we become aware of an associated feeling of fear. Understanding how these mechanisms normally work will have important consequences for how we manage our knowledge acquisition and deployment processes.

Work is inherently an emotional experience. Emotions are intrinsic to our essence and cannot be artificially segregated between our personal lives (where feelings are allowed) and our professional activities (where cold logic is preferred). Neurologists recently located emotional processing in certain prefrontal areas of the brain called the amygdala. Individuals who suffer damage in this area have great difficulty maintaining a sense of responsibility for themselves, for others and for planning their future as social beings. They know but cannot feel. Their logical reasoning skills and memory, which holds their knowledge base, are intact and performing well – some even have above average IQs. This enables them to analyze various alternatives with great lucidity and detail – but they can neither select one option nor act upon it. They have the ability to prioritize and make decisions on personal and social matters where choices involve incomplete or inadequate data. As a result, their adaptability skills in complex social environments have been severely diminished.[6]

" Our brains can detect danger before we even experience the feeling of being afraid"

The almost separate ability to create feelings, emotions and actions can lead to the disruptive process that we often experience when trying to manage our knowledge acquisition and storage process. The connections between the amygdala and the neocortex are the hub of the battles between head and heart. The emotional centre of the brain has a direct link to the part that processes the working memory and, as a result, strong feelings of anxiety and anger can create neural static, damaging the ability to manage knowledge contained in the short-term memory. Thus, when trying to deal with a problem, we often experience the frustration of not being able to put things into order or make sense of what appears to be a relatively simple problem.

The amygdala can also influence the memory in other ways. The physical linkage between the emotional centre and the memory system seems to allow emotions to impact upon the strength of storage. As we store and recall those moments of high anxiety, we often remember those moments of intense pleasure or happiness. The more intense the amygdala arousal, the stronger the imprint. This means that the brain has in fact two virtual memory systems, one for ordinary facts and a special system for emotional memories.

The danger with this is that the memory might be stuck in a time warp – promoting that certain thoughts and ideas are valid, when in fact an environmental shift means that they are obsolete. It can create a situation where people respond to a current problem based upon schemata that were imprinted a long time ago. Hence we act and apply knowledge in a way that rationally seems inappropriate, but we still carry on delivering the ideas regardless.

The other problem is that emotional memory can offer an imperfect bias on a situation. Even though a memory of a situation is felt to be strong and accurate, the schematic filters that are incorporated in the memory can create a bias. Emotional memories are not (like some people like to think) carbon copies of what actually happened. They are reconstructions of a personal event and are being replayed through multiple biases and filters, the majority of which we are not even aware of. Compare two opposing football supporters describing the match they watched together. Split them into separate rooms and the whole replay of the match would be heavily biased by their mood on the day of the match, their mood at the time of replay, their bias for their team and a wide host of different emotional factors.

Social capital

One important question to consider is: Can knowledge be stored collectively across a group of people? This is often referred to as 'organizational memory' or social capital – the place where everything contained in the organization is somehow retrievable.[7] This refers to the amount of stored knowledge and experience held within the individual or organization. As an example, an organization that has been working in a particular industry for a while is likely to have accumulated a high level of declarative knowledge about the competitive structure and detailed traits of the industry. This knowledge will be found in the minds of the people who operate the business, but you will probably find knowledge representation in the way that products and services are designed to meet the market requirements. Although there is some debate as to the extent to which organizations can store memory like individuals, there is a growing sense that organizations do have frames of reference, routines, structures and other artefacts that reflect stored knowledge.[8]

" The synergy that occurred when John Lennon met Paul McCartney was a form of knowledge capital that might not have occurred in any other situation "

It is important to point out that organizational capabilities are not just embedded in any single person, but in the links across diverse individual capabilities. Learning in organizations entails not only the acquisition of diverse information, but also the ability to share common understanding so as to exploit it.[9] So the synergy that occurred when John Lennon met Paul McCartney was a form of knowledge capital that might not have occurred in any other situation. This is essential value that is generated from the social or emotional interaction that occurs within a relationship. This might be defined as a source of knowledge that emerges from their 'social ties' and people's membership of certain 'communities'.

This is how organizations build and retain their advantage through the dynamic and complex interrelationships between social and personal capital.[10] The end result is a soft currency that enables an organization to operate more effectively. This includes intangible factors such as values, norms, attitudes, trust, networks and the like. It will be facilitated by those factors, found within a community, that facilitate coordination and co-operation for mutual benefit. This means that if one works in a community that has trust, values, open networks and the like, then there is a greater chance the new knowledge will emerge from the process of interaction between the members.

This stresses the need to understand and develop a high level of social capital within an organization – which is the ability of people to work together for a common purpose.[11] Francis Fukuyama considers this idea from a different direction. He believes 'the vitality of social capital is essential to the functioning of both the market and democracy'.[12] Hence, social capital might be defined as the sum of the actual and potential resources embedded within, available through and derived from the network of relationships possessed by an individual or social unit.[13] It is through the definition and management of these social relationships that knowledge can be discovered.

In a network economy, my value is directly proportional to the size and quality of my personal network. Hence, people's capacity to create new relational knowledge will be determined by the size of their relationship networks, the sum of their shared knowledge and how successfully (quickly) they can use the relationships. Hence managers with more social capital are likely to get higher returns on their human capital because they are positioned to identify and develop more opportunities.[14] The value comes from our ability to coordinate others – knowledge of who to pull together to develop new opportunities. Although personal capital is necessary for success, it can be useless without the social capital of opportunities in which to apply it.

One factor that impacts upon your ability to create or discover new knowledge is your position within the social structure. In any organization, certain people are connected to certain others, trusting certain others, obliged to support certain others and dependent on exchange with others. Your position in this complex exchange structure can be an asset in its own right. This asset is the value of social capital. Hence much of the value embedded in the social capital will be grounded in your ability to manage effective brokerage relations.[15] Intriguingly, the variable that has most impact on the value of an individual's social capital is not the number of links that an individual has, but rather the degree of competition within the social environment. If we work with peers who are prepared to undercut us within the internal market system, then our ability to discover knowledge using social relationships will be eroded.

As this diffusion occurs within an organization so we can see the growth and value of social capital in the community's ability to manage the speed and transfer of knowledge.[16] One might consider that it is the social construction of knowledge that is potentially most valuable in creating personal capital within the business. The synthesis that emerges following an interaction between two people, or groups, will bear the real fruits of the future.

● Fixed delay

When looking at software support for knowledge management, we must first consider the five main information management activities that are the core of the processes which underpin knowledge management. Essentially, these five activities are:

- collecting – pulling in information; searching for requisite knowledge, inputting data to the knowledge base;

- storing – creating indexes for information; linking data elements to highlight relationships within the information content; filtering information to weed out redundant, duplicate or non-relevant information;

- synthesizing – creating new knowledge domains;

- disseminating – pushing out information; publishing information for target groupings; notifying interest groups of updates, new research, general awareness;

- collaborating – sharing knowledge individually, or across groups.

The software available in the knowledge management arena is increasing in its functionality as well as its ability to create a more integrated and enhanced software environment. To all intents, the software covering information management can be grouped under six generic headings:

- document management systems

- information management systems

- expert systems

- search and index systems

- collaborative and communications-based systems

- intellectual asset management systems.

The early document management software was oriented towards emulating library and paper-based environments and so was focused on the collection, storage and distribution of documents. Increasingly, document management software provides a comprehensive range of capabilities including the maintenance of version control, as well as authentication and translation facilities.

The software solutions covering information management are most widely used in the management of data storage facilities such as large data warehouses, database environments and more localized data marts. However, the development of ERP (Enterprise Resource Planning) software environments (for example as represented by SAP), is beginning to have an impact on the shape of knowledge management within companies. There are also a number of software products emerging in the market which provide so-called data transformation facilities. Such software solutions focus on transforming the format of information, for example data which is held in 'legacy' application systems and old style flat files (i.e. not in a relational form). By using such software solutions, the 'legacy' information can be made more accessible to all users by transforming the information into a more accessible, intelligent relational database environment.

The development and application of expert systems has meant that in some areas of information management data can be used in a more knowledgeable and useful way. The expert system is built to provide an intelligent analysis of information linked with data filtering facilities and packaged with an on-line processing capability. The expert system will sift through large amounts of data to ensure that the information retrieved is useful to the user and the organization.

In essence, the expert systems software solutions are used to emulate specific decision-making processes within an organization, where the organization believes that the collection and synthesis of information in a controlled environment enables decisions to be taken without human intervention. For example, many of the leading financial institutions use expert systems to validate loan applications.

Within the search and index field of software provision, the greatest impetus for development has been the Internet where there has been a huge demand for sophisticated search and indexing software from a vast range of Internet users, service providers and web sites. The massive growth in information and the demand to link differing systems, sites, facilities, etc. has meant that there is an almost bewildering array of software on the market to handle this particular need.

A key element in any knowledge management initiative is providing a means of communicating and collaborating which facilitates the flow of information, particularly the dissemination of tacit knowledge. Indeed, the issue of precisely how tacit knowledge is incorporated into the knowledge management environment is a key and differentiating factor between knowledge management and information management systems.

There are a number of 'group-ware' software facilities which are used by large international organizations to link diverse and dispersed users and entities together through a common information and communications framework. Used in this way, such systems can provide a powerful collaborative impetus within an organization. However, it is interesting to note that even with all the knowledge and information which is held electronically, the sum total of individual and business knowledge residing outside the electronic environment still vastly outweighs the electronic content.

The development of intellectual asset management systems has not seen the explosive growth seen with some of the other software areas discussed previously. This is primarily due to much of the software being developed 'internally' and most of it emanating from the legal companies sector. For those companies using such software, the concentration has been on tracking the intellectual assets of the company such as contracts, trademarks, patents, legal cases and precedents. However, we can see that with the mushrooming interest in all things to do with the Web, many innovative organizations will want to have such software available to maintain their intellectual asset libraries.

So where does all of this leave us? In a sense it does mean that most knowledge management practitioners and organizations have to assemble a varying range of software products in order to create the knowledge management environment they are seeking. And, at this point in time, there does not appear to be a single, unifying vendor who can provide the total solution to meet the knowledge management software aspirations of an organization.

As a result, you need to make choices about what systems can be used to store, disseminate and recall information as and when you need it. Although the capability to manage and exploit your personal capital is not dependent upon the use of technology and software, the chances are that those who have a good appreciation of its value and application will be able to better exploit their intellectual capital.

> *"The sum total of individual and business knowledge residing outside the electronic environment still vastly outweighs the electronic content"*

Choose the right storage process

So, you have discovered this great new idea! The first choice you have to make is should you take it to market that instant (like a street trader or ticket tout) or does it have to go into the delay routine. If you need to take the delay option, the question is then how will you store the knowledge.

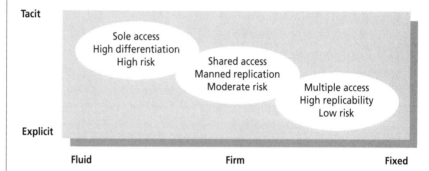

Figure 7.8

After all the various options are considered, it often boils down to one of three choices: the fluid option, whereby you hold it inside yourself; the firm option, whereby you partially codify the knowledge, but record it in a system that is personal to you; or you can take the fixed option and hard code it into a system, process or report.

No one delay process is right, as the decisions around this stage will be depend upon the content of the knowledge and the context in which it is being stored. However, they do come with various risks for both you and the organization you work with. The fluid choice keeps power with the knowledge owner and allows you to leverage personal gain from the asset base. However, the risk for you is that you might forget it and the risk to the organization is that when you walk out the door so does the personal capital. The second option might be that you make a rough note in a diary or log book. This gives you the security that it will be easier to recall at a later date, but you are starting to hand over control of the capital of the knowledge, especially if the log book system is owned by another person or company. The final option is to opt for the fixed storage.

While this guarantees the information will be there for others to access (unless password protected), it can reduce your capital value and reduces your personal market value.

Although there is no right answer for this conundrum, there might be a right question. If you are originating knowledge and publishing this as information for others to see, then ensure that the ideas offered in the delivery section of the book are considered. Ensure that you receive the reward that you believe is appropriate. Although the delay stage is concerned with storage, by virtue of the fact that your knowledge has been codified and made open, you might be at risk of delivering market value for little market return.

Delay questions

- To what extent do you understand how you store and delay knowledge that is not currently in use?

- What is your primary, explicit head knowledge that you can call upon to create a market value?

- What explicit and tacit skills do you have in reserve?

- How quickly and readily can you access information that is stored on your hard systems?

- To what extent do you split your storage between hard and human systems?

- Do you understand how to maximize the effectiveness of your short-term or working memory?

- To what extent do your emotions impact upon the storage and retrieval process?

- How do you know if your memories have not been overly biased and corrupted by the emotional effect during storage?

- Do you take time to replay and watch your episodic memories so as to enable the recall process at a later date?

- To what extent do you have social capital with colleagues and friends – how retrievable is it?

- Do you know what rehearsal process can be used to retain knowledge in your working memory?

- Do you know what associative techniques help to transfer knowledge to your long-term memory?

- Do you have personal techniques for chunking knowledge so as to increase the storage of the working memory?

- What fixed systems do you have to store your knowledge and how effective are they?

- Are you storing personal information that others can use to create market value?

8

Knowledge disposal

In Time Of Profound Change, The Learners Inherit The Earth,
While The Learned Find Themselves Beautifully Equipped To Deal
With A World That No Longer Exists.

Al Rogers

Given the increasing pace of change, it is difficult to set up defined models of the future. All the suggestions are that we are moving into more eclectic times. These times will probably defy the 'predictive and deterministic' nature of traditional information systems, control systems and performance systems and put an increasing premium on ongoing learning and, more critically, the process of unlearning. The old mechanistic and static world has now fallen by the wayside, as evidenced by the cyberspace-based emergent phenomena affecting businesses, industries, governments and the global society at large. If we accept that change is now the norm then, as individuals, we must learn to adapt and let go of that which existed yesterday. Hence, the process of unlearning is one that is required in a world of rampant change. If we are to match and master our environment, then we must develop the ability to discard old ways and knowledge as well as acquiring new ones.

If knowledge is compared to stock, then at some stage the old and redundant stockpile will have to be replenished. This need to constantly update and refine the knowledge base is something that is becoming increasingly important as the pace of life speeds up. One clear example of this is the initiative started by Jack Welch in GE Capital. Under the heading 'destroyyourbusiness.com', Jack urged his team to destroy their previous business model before someone else does. With the rampant increase in e-business, he recognized that the disposal process is key to letting go of old and taking on new ways of thinking and working.[1]

Shere Hite, in her book *Sex and Business*, offers a simple example of the disposal process. She uses a computer analogy, on the assumption that people can learn to delete old software and install new ways of thinking or feeling. For example, she suggests the following.

● **Software to delete**. Women are inferior. Women are not made for business, but for love and sex.

● **Software to install**. Women, like men, have many sides to their personalities and identity. Women vary.[2]

This example suggests a shift in the way that sexual bias can be approached within organizations. Clearly, we can accept new ideas and ways of working, but before we do this we have to let go of the past and lose the old way of thinking.

Dispose matrix

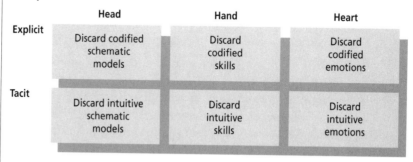

Figure 8.1

Explicit head

This is the capability to let go and erase current models and mental frameworks that you knowingly use to make decisions. One example might be the shift from one operating process to another, or the decision to move from a paper-based time management system to an electronic tool.

Explicit hand

This is the ability to discard unwanted or redundant skills and capabilities. This might be seen in someone who has immigrated to a new country where people drive on the opposite side of the road. There will have to be a fairly rapid and controlled ability to change a specific set of skills, such as where the gear stick and rear view mirrors are and how to take a right hand turn.

Explicit heart

This is the ability to let go of known emotions. This might (as experienced by so many people) be the change we go through when experiencing a divorce or retirement. In essence it is about managing an emotion that is related to the intra or interpersonal element of your life.

Tacit head

With this component, the objective is to erase those guiding frameworks that implicitly drive how you act and make decisions. This might be changing how you feel about a particular group of individuals or branch of an organization. One personal example is when I transferred from an engineering group to a sales function. So often these two groups are at war with each other because of their separate goals and values. I had been unknowingly ingrained with the view that sales people were difficult to get on with and not willing to look after the customer's aims. Only after I had been in sales for a few months did my viewpoint change, although I didn't realize that the shift had happened until a few years later.

Tacit hand

In this case the action is to give up a specific set of behaviours or actions that no longer create value in the market. Nowhere is this more apparent than in the shift towards e-commerce. Barely an organization can sit back and argue that the electronic changes being fostered by the growth of the Internet will not impact upon their business. However, this change goes deeper than just new technical and functional skills. With the increase in remote working, managers need to learn a new set of deep skills. No longer can they measure output and value on the hours their team works, as in many cases the team members will be invisible. We need to let go of a management skill where the leader commands and controls the team and instead must develop new leadership and management capabilites.

Tacit heart

This is the ability to let go of deeply held relationships and passion that are no longer valid in the current world. This might be akin to the shift that you have to make when letting go of an old relationship – with a person or a company. Of all the six aspects of the dispose stage, I suggest that this one is probably the most difficult to undertake. As anyone who has been dumped as a teenager will recognize, simply telling your feelings to go away can be almost impossible. This is often dependent upon support and time – these help us to go through what can be a quite traumatic closure stage. This issue can be seen in many companies where people are unwilling to let go of the legacy of past greatness. Look at any large ex-government organization; although it will have gone through substantial functional changes in the shift to a market orientation, the biggest hurdle will always be that people hark back to the 'good old days'.

Of all the stages in the flow model this is the ball-buster, it is the one that we often find difficult to deal with. Aren't we all supposed to accumulate knowledge, shouldn't we aspire to grab everything we can and isn't it right to go on every course that we can to grow our personal capital? Maybe, but if you find it difficult to hold on to conflicting views at any one time then you have to develop the capability to let go of ideas that no longer add value. To achieve this, you might need to ask yourself the following questions.

- Have I developed my capability to unlearn?
- How do I manage the pain that goes with letting go?
- What strategies do I have to ensure that I let go on my terms rather than being forced by someone else?

Unless you understand how to manage your capability in these three areas, then you might be seen as someone who lives in the past and is unable to accept new ways of thinking, feeling and behaving.

Unlearning – the great unspoken

Imagine, a plane comes in to land at Heathrow airport and all of a sudden the pilot announces that the undercarriage is stuck and the plane will have to make an emergency landing. As the plane lands, the passengers are instructed to leave the plane rapidly, as a fire may break out. What will people do in this situation? The rational view is that they will quickly leave without waiting to unpack their luggage from the overhead locker – the reality is, in many crashes, people put their lives at risk by waiting to get their possessions out of the overhead rack.

The reason for this behaviour is that we still follow the mental map or schema programmed for a normal landing. We have not been able to release or quickly unlearn the process that exists in our heads for ordinary departure from the aeroplane. The standard map is that upon landing, people stand up and wait to get their possessions and only once this task is achieved can they leave the plane. However, in an emergency, speed is of the essence and the quickest person out of the plane stands the great-est chance of survival. The evidence is that those who survive are those who ignore the existing schemata or self-imposed rules and look for ways to circumvent the standard ways of exiting.

"Simply letting go of knowledge is not always as easy as it sounds"

In the same way that we must learn how to learn, we must learn how to unlearn – to be able to let go of knowledge that is of no further use. This is not the same as throwing away knowledge. The brain doesn't erase memories, it changes the connections, renewing some, letting others fade away, under a form of selection. When we remember we recreate mem-ories, based on those strengthened or weakened connections. In order to recast our knowledge, we have to throw away the old pattern.[3]

However, simply letting go of knowledge is not always as easy as it sounds. The simple fact that knowledge is associated with power, prestige and political clout means that we are often loath to simply release it for others to use. In addition, unlearning is emotionally difficult because the old way of doing things has worked for a while and become embedded in our beliefs and behaviours.[4] We have to shift from the comfortable domain in the existing organizational environment and be prepared to migrate to the new form. This is based on the premise that we will be able to discard and forgo any existing mental models that might have held the status quo. This can be difficult because we often remain prisoners of our conceptual framework, where there is a general reluctance to leave the old way of thinking.[5]

It is also important to understand the difference between the disposal of process and of content. We need to distinguish between unlearning what we know and do, from how we learn. If we simply get rid of old content but continue to follow inappropriate or redundant learning strategies, then all we will do is replenish the stock with old knowledge. Conversely, we might let go of redundant ways of learning and as a result lose access to valuable data sources that cannot be accessed via any other route. The goal is that we make informed assessments about how present capabilities realize or inhibit learning and whether barriers to improved performance exist because of what is being learned versus how learning occurs.[6]

This suggests that the disposal process is critical to the learning process. However, the proposition is that it is rarely considered. In a scan of the leading KM articles, very few of them explicitly consider the notion of redundant knowledge and how it might be managed out of the system. Unless we learn how to let go of past and redundant knowledge, then we will find it difficult to accept and embrace new forms of knowledge.

Letting go

It is entirely normal for individuals, teams, organizations or even nations to react adversely when they have to dispose of a current knowledge. This reaction can be mapped in the form of a chart – one that maps time against the emotional stages you might pass through, as seen in Fig. 8.2. The U-loop is a powerful and effective change model that clearly maps many of the feelings associated with change and learning. We especially feel these emotions where the change process affects self-esteem or position in an organization. The suggestion is that there are five major stages in the process of change.[7]

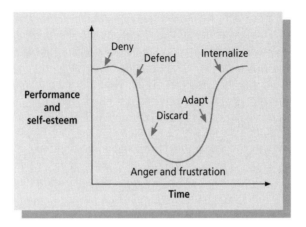

Figure 8.2
Change U-loop

Deny

We often feel uncomfortable with change. The typical response to any variation is to ignore it. People either do not believe that it will affect them or are resigned to the idea that there is nothing they can do, so it is best to ignore the threat.

Defend

This is where we might take action to try to prevent the change from taking place. It might be simply withdrawing from the process or in some extremes taking pre-meditated guerrilla or political action to stop the change from happening.

Discard

Change is about shifting our schema or map of the world. To move forward, we have to discard past behaviours, feelings and consequences; to let go and be happy with what has gone.

Adapt

At this point the past has been left behind so we can begin to explore new ways of working. This is a confusing time, as the old and new are still likely to be in conflict with each other. However, with the correct support processes in place, we can quickly shift to the next stage of commitment.

● Internalize

Once the change has been accepted, we can adopt it as the norm and internalize it as the current way of operating. At this point the energy returns, the process is owned and the individual will, in many cases, try to convince others of its benefits.

These stages can be found in all situations where old ways of working, thinking and feeling are challenged, for instance the way that we react to a change in our job description; the suggestion that it is time to lose some weight; or the pain associated with enforced redundancy. Although each example is different, all the players will follow the pattern outlined in the U-loop.

One example of this was the production of the Sony Walkman. During the 1970s, the Sony Corporation produced a small, portable, monaural tape recorder. It was named the Pressman because Sony expected reporters to use it to record interviews. In 1978, the engineers who developed the Pressman tried to upgrade it to stereo sound. They succeeded in squeezing the components needed for stereo playback into the Pressman's chassis. But there was no room left for recording components, so the engineers were left with a recorder that could not record. Unsure what to do, the engineers dropped the project and used the unsuccessful prototype to play background music in their laboratory.

Sony's founder in 1946 had been Masaru Ibuka. Although Ibuka had retired, he was called Sony's Honorary Chairman and he had the habit of occasionally roaming around the laboratories and factories. One of these tours took Ibuka into the laboratory where the tape recorder engineers were playing their unsuccessful prototype. 'And then one day, into our room came Mr Ibuka, our Honorary Chairman. He just popped into the room, saw us listening to this and thought it was very interesting.' Ibuka said he thought the small box was producing excellent sound. He asked if they had considered producing a machine that had no recording capability. Also, he suggested that if the machine had no speaker, its batteries would last much longer. He had just visited another Sony laboratory where someone had developed very small headphones that might be mated to this non-recording recorder.

Engineers and managers in both the tape recorder division and the headphone division saw no merit in Ibuka's idea. A tape recorder that lacked both a speaker and recording capability was no recorder at all, so no one would buy it. Headphones were merely a supplement to loudspeakers; if a device had only headphones, only one person could listen.

Undeterred, Ibuka went to Sony's real Chairman, Akio Morita and said: 'Let's put together one of these things and try it. Let's see how it sounds.' So a machine was assembled and both Ibuka and Morita liked the way it sounded.

Morita decided that Sony should put the Walkman into production. This made the managers of the tape recorder division quite unhappy because, as they saw it, they were being ordered to produce an ineffective device that would almost certainly lose money. With the new lightweight headphones, it would cost $249. Not only was this more expensive than tape recorders with speakers that could record, but the expected teenage consumers could not possibly spend more than $170. The marketing managers said bluntly, 'This is a dumb idea.' Morita declared that the price would be $165 and he told the tape recorder division to make 60,000 of them.

The managers of the tape recorder division judged that they were being commanded to lose $35 per unit sold. 'There was no profit. The more we produced, the more we lost.' They secretly decided to produce only 30,000 units and they allotted a marketing budget of only $100,000.

Sony sold almost no Walkmans during the first month after the product's introduction. Then sales picked up and during the third month, sales rocketed . . . until Sony ran out of inventory. That was when Morita found out that the tape recorder division had produced only 30,000 instead of 60,000. The tape recorder division quickly corrected its error. Six months after the product's introduction, Sony was producing and selling 30,000 units per month.[8]

This case study highlights how even experienced experts can find it difficult to let go of previous ways of thinking. No one should be confident that their current beliefs and methods are optimal. Optimality is unlikely. If beliefs seem accurate, someone else is probably finding other beliefs equally effective. If methods seem excellent today, better methods will appear tomorrow. Thus, you are well-advised to remain ever sceptical. 'It isn't good enough' and 'It's only an experiment' are mental frameworks that help one stay constantly alert for opportunities to improve. 'It isn't good enough' reminds one to look for more accurate beliefs or better methods. 'It's only an experiment' helps one to feel less committed to current beliefs and methods.

Dispose strategy

The way we let go of knowledge will depend on the content and context of the situation. However, there are two consistent variables that will impact upon the strategy you might follow in the disposal process. The first is the extent to which the need to lose knowledge is either a forced or a voluntary action; the second is the extent to which the disposal is unplanned or planned. A combination of these two variables will produce the table shown in Fig. 8.3.

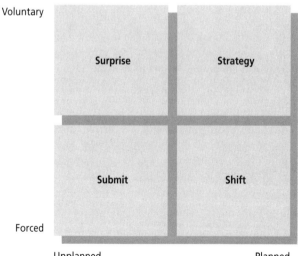

Figure 8.3

Submit

The forced/unplanned disposal process is one where knowledge has to be disposed of and the owner has little advance warning or choice in the matter. This happened to large numbers of people during the sudden corporate urge to downsize organizations. One day you might be contentedly managing a process, product or project and then along comes the process reengineering culture and bang, you're out of a job. This change left many people in the position where they had to undertake a rapid reorientation of their knowledge base. Often, in this situation, the forced disposal can be painful, but people's ability to erase the past is enhanced by their personal motivation to acquire knowledge in order to get a new source of income.

Surprise

In this quadrant, the disposal process is voluntary and under the control of the individual, but the timing is not known. This can be akin to the situation where someone has bid for a place on a training course, but doesn't know what date he or she will be allocated. Although the timing of the disposal process may be fluid, the fact that they have made a personal choice to dispose of old knowledge does make it easier both to erase the content and to acquire new skills and ideas.

Shift

This is a forced, but planned knowledge disposal. This might be the case of someone who develops an illness, which means she can no longer work under the same pressure she has been experiencing in recent years. So although she knows that the current knowledge base will be redundant, she still has time in which to dispose of the current platform and create a new knowledge base that will enable her to earn a living, but at a more relaxed pace.

Strategy

This type of disposal can be seen when someone knows they are about to make a significant career switch. Imagine the money broker who decides to give up the life of banking and become a mushroom farmer. He knows that at some point the knowledge will be redundant and so has time to prepare for the shift and space to develop the appropriate strategies that will allow him to forgo the current knowledge platform.

Although the disposal process will often be unplanned and forced, we should always try to shift it to the strategy box. To achieve this we have to do two things. The first is to make internal decisions that 'other people will not force me to change. Although they might initiate the stimulus or manage the environment, ultimately I will choose to go through the U-loop and I will understand the consequences of my action.' The second is to stay attuned to the market. Don't accept that the way life is – is the way life is. Embrace and welcome the notion of change and wherever possible become its master.

To become a master of change, you must know its nature. There should be an acceptance that control, conformity and consistency are things of the past and turbulence, trauma and transition are in effect the new natural state. In understanding this nature of change, it is important that you appreciate how this shift from equilibrium to turbulence will affect your current knowledge and have a clear picture of how you might react where change rears its head. In this way, few disposal actions are likely to be unplanned as you will be forewarned and forearmed.

" To become a master of change, you must know its nature"

In maintaining the disposal stage, a sense of change mastery can be achieved – with this comes a new type of comfort and protection. Imagine that rather than disposal being a threatening and disrupting process, it can be regarded as a new form of security.[9] In the more traditional organization, security is based upon the acquisition of power: the power to hold resources, discipline people, control the finances and build personal empires. In organizations that value knowledge, your ability to let go of and acquire new knowledge will ultimately offer a greater degree of influence and control than the ability to accumulate hierarchical power.

Dispose questions

- What is the last chunk of knowledge you let go of and how did you do it?

- What will be the next chunk of knowledge that you need to dispose of?

- Which is hardest for you to dispose of: ideas, behavioural skills or emotional awareness?

- What deep or tacit ideas are you not prepared to let go of and why?

- What strategies do you have to manage yourself through the U-loop?

- What is the last way of working that your team or organization discarded?

- What strategies do you have for looking into the future to understand what changes are coming?

- What personal strategies do you have for taking control when others try to impose change on you?

- Do you have an archive process to lose emotional attachment to knowledge but to retain it for later retrieval?

9

Knowledge diffusion

In every man there is something wherein I may learn of him and in that I am his pupil.

Ralph Waldo Emerson

Consider a country that has a series of fast interconnecting trains and roads, then consider another where the framework is made up of single-track lanes and a run-down, ill-equipped railway system. Both countries might have companies that are investing in new plant and infrastructure, but without a tight, fast and smooth network, little growth will happen. In the same way, an organization can invest fortunes in its asset base, but if we are not able to talk, share ideas and create knowledge through internalization and synthesis, only limited improvement will emerge from the capital investment.

Knowledge diffusion is about sharing schemata through the process of collaborative and challenging interactions. It is the process of sharing knowledge where the goal is to enhance or improve the value and quality of the content rather than to barter or trade its value in the open market. Although the process of diffusion will include a degree of trade as we offer ideas and feedback on our thoughts, the primary difference with the delivery stage is in intent – your goal is not to create a market value, rather it is to enhance the value of the existing knowledge.

Diffuse matrix

	Head	Hand	Heart
Explicit	Share ideas through a codified process	Share skills through a codified process	Share emotions through a codified process
Tacit	Share ideas through association	Share skills through association	Share emotions through association

Figure 9.1

Explicit head

This is how we share the models and frameworks that help us function and take decisions. This is one of the more common activities seen inside organizations. Examples of this type of diffusion can be a brainstorming session; team meetings; or report submissions – where the aim is to use a range of codified elements to share and sometimes amplify knowledge within a defined community.

Explicit hand

Here the goal is to share the explicit skills and physical competencies that you might have. Examples might be the last time you asked someone how to wire up a plug, change a spark plug, or operate a piece of machinery. These are skills that can be clearly explained and the owner has a good understanding of what they are and how they can be applied in the market.

Explicit heart

If you share your explicit emotions, then you will be helping others to take on board some of your soft skills. This might be how you build relationships, motivate yourself, or influence and coach other people. The primary point is that you can make explicit for others how you manage your inter- and intra-personal emotions.

Tacit head

With this you are sharing your deep schemata and mental models used to dictate the decisions you make and how you make them. Consider the way that you prepare and deliver a product presentation to a management team. The way you dress, the words you use, the style used to build the slides all indicate certain deep beliefs and ideas that you use to manage yourself. On the first presentation, the receivers might not adopt this mental model, but over time there is a chance that other people will adopt some of your personal preferences and style.

Tacit hand

The skills that you use to offer your ideas might be based upon some degree of formal training, but can also indicate a deeper level of tacit ability. For me, I now find that my capability to develop, to read and work the audience at a music gig helps me when I am working with teams in a training environment.

Tacit heart

Finally, let's look at the presentation example again. In putting forward an argument, you might deliberately use some explicit emotion to emphasize and sell certain points, but underneath that, your deep beliefs about the product will probably show through. Your deep emotions will softly and intuitively inform the audience of your feelings about the idea and will often greatly impact upon their final view of you, the presentation and the product being offered.

Once the knowledge has been acquired, it can be shared with others through a process of diffusion (possibly to enhance its value). This might be through involvement with a colleague to prepare a paper; presentation to the management board; or inclusion on an intranet site. In many ways, it is at this stage of the framework that the organizational learning and knowledge management ethos starts to shine through.

To understand your capability and desire to operate in this stage of the flow model, you might ask the following questions.

- What explicit and intuitive processes do I use to share and exchange knowledge with colleagues?
- To what extent do competitive forces impact on my ability or desire to share knowledge?
- To what extent do I manage knowledge as a tradable entity?
- How do I use the uncharted communities to amplify and enhance my personal capital?

The whole economic, managerial and academic thrust behind the knowledge management initiative is on the presumption that, for an organization to survive and adapt, it must be able to share knowledge within the organization. If new knowledge stays with one person then any opportunity to enhance the value of the organization will be limited. I suggest that the relationship between individual and organizational learning is related in part to your power to facilitate and drive the diffusion process. To this end, you must make the dynamics and issues surrounding the diffusion process open, discussible and actionable.

X-change model

If we accept that the knowledge will be transferred at either explicit or tacit level, then the four types of exchange shown in Fig. 9.2 might be considered.

Explain – Explicit to explicit

Diffusion at this level is something we all do, everyday, without any real thought or question. When we write a letter, prepare a report, or enter data on a database, we are sharing our explicit knowledge with other people. Look at anyone's diary and you will see ample examples of the diffusion process at this level. Look again in the diary and you will find examples of tacit diffusion, but it will probably be marginal activities, such as social engagements, evening meetings in the wine bar, or a reminder to meet someone for coffee.

The primary goal in diffusing explicit knowledge is to systemize concepts

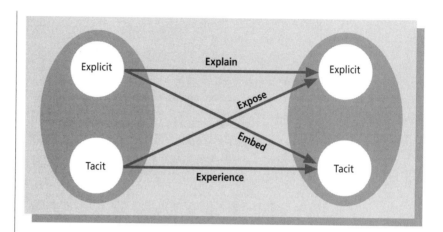

Figure 9.2
Diffusion
framework

into shared schemata. This can be achieved through a process of incorp-oration and separation. As your information flows with others, it will be synthesized, modified and generally played with until it takes on a new and original form. Think about the construction of a management report. Although one person might have written the document, it will generally be grounded in a stream of debate that has taken place over the preced-ing weeks and months. So the end explicit product is actually the product of an explicit diffusion process that occurred prior to the event.

'Explain' is often the primary process by which companies communicate corporate messages within organizations. The company newsletter, chair-man's web site, or the mugs promoting new company vision are all examples of the explicit to explicit process of diffusion. Although explicit communication clearly has its strengths (for example, telling someone that a ladder is about to fall on their head) when the message needs to have a sense of passion and feeling, then the explicit process does have its limi-tations. One of the ways that companies are starting to overcome this is through the use of web broadcasts to promote company messages. As com-pany intranet bandwidths increase so will the capacity to use web-cams and video broadcasts to promote some of the softer communications aspects. Although not quite to a tacit level, the use of interactive tools and emotional images can help to ease the explanation process.

Although this form of diffusion can be commonly seen, the problem is that behind every piece of codified information will be the tacit knowledge of the original creator. Only by appreciating the tacit intent of the creator will you be able to realize the intended value. It is dangerous to assume that the message you read will be the same as the message someone writes. For example, as I write these words now, trying to get them onto the page can be quite torturous, as I struggle to make sense of the tacit ideas and emotions that drive their construction. Even as I write I don't really know what will come out next. Wrapped around these words is a blanket of tacit thoughts and feelings, ones that, unfortunately, you are unable to see. As such, as you read them you will be filtering, critiquing and judging the words, rather than truly understanding what I mean. We all see the world through our perceptual filters and in the majority of cases we find it difficult to know what those filters are, let alone describe how they corrupt any information we acquire.

Another problem with explicit to explicit diffusion is the ease with which it can be communicated. The introduction of e-mail and the cc button has probably caused more time management problems for people than all the other business issues put together. It seems that we often go crazy with the power to be able to copy the world in on our latest note. Whereas pre e-mail, we would have had to walk to the photocopier, put the paper in an envelope and then post a whole wodge of envelopes, now that one button can flood the company in seconds with spurious and occasionally irritating messages. As a result we are now in the era of information overload. Barely a train journey goes by when I don't hear people bemoaning (or bragging) about how much e-mail they received overnight.

One button can flood the company in seconds with spurious and occasionally irritating messages

The end result of all this data rush is that the discovery stage becomes clogged up, primarily with data that has little relevance to one's personal value proposition. As a result, we often spend more and more time in the explicit diffusion activities, all of which contributes to the fact that less time is spent on those tacit transfer activities that can add real personal value.

This focus on explicit to explicit diffusion is often reinforced by the performance management systems that companies adopt. It never fails to surprise me just how many people measure their personal value to the business by the number of e-mails they initiate or how many management reports they produce. It also never fails to surprise me just how many companies fail to recognize and reward the value that is accumulated if we are allowed time to enhance our tacit value. Often people seen talking at the coffee machine or having a cigarette break together are badged as slackers, when they may be helping to diffuse some of the deeper tacit knowledge that resides within the business.

Finally, the explicit to explicit process is crucial, yet it is not the only one. The difficulty is in trying to achieve an effective balance between this diffusion method and the other three. Too much emphasis on this method will result in a highly codified flow of information that can be copied and replicated in the market. Too little will result in an organization that is only able to share through highly associative methods and relationships.

Embed – Explicit to tacit

This is how our explicit knowledge is taken and internalized by another person or group of people. For example this embedding process is often seen in the indoctrination courses used by large consulting firms. The goal is to take the company methodology and attempt to embed it into the new recruits deep tacit systems. So the new employees have all entered with their different disciplinary backgrounds and the course director's role is to mould the group to a point where they will think, feel and behave in a way that underpins and reinforces the company ethos and methodology.

In many cases you might embed capability in others through the use of stories and analogies. For example, Xerox is effective at repairing copiers, not primarily because it has good manuals and good training courses. It is effective mainly because it has a group of repair people of varying degrees of mastery who constantly share with each other in ways that promote learning, development and effective work in the field. They use 'walkie talkies' to get instant help and to share their 'war stories' with each other so that what is developed is a corporate or community knowledge, beyond what any individual could master. IBM discovered that the best sales training was to put beginners, in their early months on the job, physically next to a respected master so that they could learn by observation and intuition as well as by explicit teaching from those people.[1]

Expose – Tacit to explicit

This is possibly one of the harder elements in the diffusion framework. The idea is to take something that I hold at a deep and intuitive level and share it with another at the explicit level. This is often a process by which I start to expose my deep beliefs about a subject – the skills that I use to get a particular sound from the bass guitar; or the emotions that I have about a certain person or subject. The end goal is to move the knowledge into a concept that can be understood and replicated by others.

However, the first problem is that the very fact that it is tacit means that I will struggle to make it explicit to myself before making it clear to others. Now it might be that through a process of inner induction and deduction I can describe the fact that I hold the guitar in a certain way; bend the string a minute fraction and then use my fingers in a certain way to provide a rich bass sound – but even then there is a chance that I am doing things that I don't understand and cannot explain. This will lead to unexplainable gaps between the tacit action and the codified explicit model.

However, there are ways that the tacit factors can be exposed and diffused. One of the first ways is through the use of storyboards. Rather than trying to talk through how you manage a process, try drawing a series of rich pictures that add up to a sequential map of the action. The way you build the picture, the items you include and the subtle nuances of the design might well help you and others to delve deeper into the tacit knowledge. Another technique can be the use of stories or metaphors. Rather than trying to describe how you manage a team of engineers, liken it to the way you repair a fault on the car or decorate the house. Through the pictorial pictures and analogies, it might be possible to expose deeper aspects of your management style. Lastly, don't try to expose what you do – ask someone else to describe what they observe. It might be that we are unable to personally deconstruct the tacit element but through a process of feedback and debate, it might possible to understand yourself through the eyes of another person.

Finally, one of the most common ways that this process can be seen in organizations, homes or down at the local bar is through the use of war stories. As people describe how they dealt with a difficult situation they are gently eliciting some of the deeper decision-making processes and strategies they use to manage problems. By carefully listening to what people say, how they say it and the outcomes of the situation, it is possible to quickly elicit someone's tacit capabilities and possibly reconstruct and apply them in a different situation.

Experience – Tacit to tacit

The tacit to tacit diffusion process is probably one of the most common but least managed processes. From early childhood we all use this framework as a way of gathering new knowledge to survive in a complex world. At school we might absorb some of the teachers' explicit knowledge, but deep down we are being conditioned (positively or negatively) by their personal views and values.

From there we move into the apprentice stage of our lives. This might be mastering the complexities of university life under the wing of a pastoral tutor. It might be part of the apprentice model where someone will spend between two and five years with a series of people who are recognized as masters in their discipline. This leads into the later years of our education, even to the point where the PhD student sits under the wing of the supervisor, or a director mentors the manager as he or she aspires to climb the corporate ladder.

The whole experience stage of this model is based upon the precept that knowledge transference can take place by association and being close to an individual rather than receiving coded signals that we choose to internalize and adopt. The experience process is driven by a number of simple precepts that are listed below.

- The receiver will absorb the other person's experiences and knowledge through a process of observation, imitation and practice. The apprentice engineer might first watch the technician wire up a complex network, then try the process under the watchful eye of the tutor and then finally be given sufficient personal space to try the action on his or her own.

- It is inherently context driven, in that when receiving information from another person, the transfer will be influenced by the setting which can, in many cases, heavily modify the absorption process. For example, the tacit knowledge a junior doctor receives from the senior consultant will be heavily dependent upon the ethical standard and operating procedures used in the hospital.

- Even though the knowledge diffusion process might be work-focused, this doesn't mean that it must occur in a work setting. The Friday night beer bust or social activities that drive an organization will offer greater opportunities to transfer tacit knowledge than those formal events that are stage managed by the organization. It is in this situation that we can build personal models about the rules of thumb and subtle guidelines that drive an industry.

- Tacit diffusion is often based on the 'if and then' model rather than the 'what to do' type of knowledge. Rather than the expert saying how to function and what decision to take in a generic sense, the experience process is often about the logical steps that we go through when faced with a problem and the different options we use to resolve the situation.

- Although the situation will change over time, the capability to diffuse experience through the use of technology is limited. By its very nature experience is associative, context-based, intuitive and grounded in the personal values of the operator. It is very difficult to truly transfer spirit, dreams and beliefs over the Internet to someone who sits hundreds of miles away.

- Often the diffusion process and transfer of experience will take place without the recipient's knowledge. Consider how you might play sport with others and over time start to adopt features of another person without taking a conscious decision to do so. I know that the way that I play guitar will be driven by the natural style of the person that I am playing with. Even to the point that when I go back to perform with someone who I used to play with, the first few sessions can be uncomfortable as I try to adjust to someone else's natural rhythm and technique.

● Where the diffusion is managed, there will be a currency trade of some sort. The master is effectively giving away secrets and currency that a potential competitor will be able to use in the market. While the exchange might not be of a monetary value, often the trade is in the form of feedback and recognition that the donor will receive from the recipient of the knowledge.

● The activity can be highly semantic and grounded in the dialogue that occurs in the act of diffusion. At best the semantic undercurrents that drive any business will be complex and at times they will be difficult to unfathom. If one looks more deeply at the relationships that fuel the tacit to tacit process, one will start to find minutiae of differences that seem imperceptible to the observer, but mean everything to the players. The nuance or tone that sales directors might use with their teams can indicate specific actions and ideas that cannot be codified in an explicit framework. The way they phrase the word 'customer' can indicate potential sales opportunities, problems and risk, along with a myriad of other details, but their team members might not be able to explain how they receive the coded signals, it is just part of the style and undercurrent that the director has embedded in the team over time.

One area where the experience style of diffusion can be seen is in the legal industry. Consider the role of the law and the way that knowledge is transferred within the profession. Although the content of the law is highly codified and explicit in nature, the interpretation and management of the law as a process is a highly tacit and intuitive process. Although, there are courses at law school on trial advocacy, legal research and legal reasoning, these courses often fall short because there is no single agreement as to the best way to analyze a problem or develop a legal argument. As a result the transference of practical legal knowledge relies upon the ad hoc nature of experience to guide junior members of the profession in the development of their expertise and competence as legal practitioners. This is because knowledge of the law is only a small part of the legal process. Legal reasoning is dependent on the ability to define, develop and deliver legal arguments that apply a favourable legal principle to a new and often diverse set of principles.[2]

Socialization issues

Organizations leverage knowledge through networks of people who collaborate – not through networks of technology. Despite endless media hype about groupware and 'interconnectivity' computer technology is not the real story. The IT graveyard is littered with companies that followed high-budget, 'visionary' chief information officers down the path of this or that client-server investment, or rolled out new e-mail systems, only to find that people still didn't want to collaborate, share and develop new knowledge. Interconnectivity begins with people who want to connect. After that, tools and technology can make the connection. Diffusion is about desire first, capability second.

However, although we might work together and spend time with each other on a social basis, this does not mean that the process of information sharing is a natural activity. The diffusion model within any community is one that is complex and driven by a number of subtle factors including:

- the level of competition within the organization;
- the idea of knowledge transacted through favour banks;
- the extent to which information is shared through communities of interest.

Competition

The idea of competition within an organization can be viewed in different ways. Some organizations create internal competition so as to manufacture creative tension and mimic the effectiveness of the external market in the internal market. Other companies believe that internal competition creates duplication, duplicity and an unnecessarily negative environment and brings the aggression and tension of the market to people who should be working together as colleagues. The reality is that it is not a black or white situation as there will always be some degree of competition between teams. Although separate groups will have their own goals and objectives, the structure of any organization will be built around the demand for financial and manpower assets and this will result in a competitive environment.

If this is the case, then the following issues might impact upon your ability to socialize ideas within a team environment.[3]

- **Within each team** – the group creates closer ties between members and is prepared to ignore previous disputes or differences. There is a shift towards a more autocratic style of management and the team emphasis shifts from friendly relationships, to more task-focused activities.

- **Between the teams** – each team will regard the other team as the enemy and will reduce the amount of communication that it extends. There is a shift in perception, with each group seeing the other in negative, stereotypical terms.

- **The winner** – the winning team may retain the sense of tightness and cohesion but can lose its sense of urgency and market awareness. The shift is from task back to personal relationships and the positive outcome encourages us to retain the stereotype's schemata that they developed during the period of confrontation.

- **The loser** – the loser might attempt to distort reality in order to see its loss in a favourable light, or find excuses. The emphasis stays on the task activities rather than the interpersonal aspects of the job and the loser works harder to win next time.

The net result in this case is that internal competition seems to provide active stimulation in certain areas, but there is some question over the total gain for the business. However, the aim here is not to consider whether competition is good or bad, but to understand its impact on the flow of knowledge.

The picture so far is that both during and after the competitive process, a split can be driven in the organization. With both teams involved in the competition and their allies being forced into separate tribal camps, a wall of confinement can be erected. The net result for the business is to hamper the knowledge creation and transfer process because:

- the walls created by the team have a negative impact on the ability of groups and individuals to effectively interact;

- reinforcement of the competitive style of management is at odds with the idea of developing synthesis through collaborative solutions;

- the intergroup tension takes the focus away from the long-term generative style of management to looking for short-term gains and solutions;

- it encourages task-based management rather than keeping a balanced perspective on the importance of managing relationships.

Competitiveness between groups is a natural part of life in a complex society. We often drift into social groups with a shared sense of purpose and degrees of rivalry can still emerge. The question that we need to consider is: How far do they amplify the natural tendency to compete and to what extent is there an overt desire to set groups against each other? If we take a decision to use competition as a way to enhance the diffusion process, we need to appreciate the potential negative factors that might be triggered.

If the process of knowledge diffusion or sharing is critical to how we enhance our personal capital, then the notion of competition needs to be understood. We cannot simply assume a tree-hugging mentality whereby it is expected that everyone will share knowledge with everyone else without question. Humans are competitive and, as such, we need to consider how the knowledge market operates and how the competitive instinct impacts upon our ability to diffuse ideas, skills and emotions.

Knowledge bank

> Well, everything in this building, everything in the criminal justice system in New York – operates on favours. Everybody does a favour for everybody else. Every chance they get, they make deposits in the Favour Bank.[4]

In the psychological system of transactional analysis, there is an established idea called Stroke Theory. This suggests that humans need to give and receive strokes or psychological stimulants that act as units of recognition.[5] For example, if someone walks down the corridor and says 'hi' to a colleague, there is an expectation that the action will receive a positive response – if nothing is forthcoming, then a sense of hurt or emptiness can be felt by the giver. The result is that next time the same person is passed, the giver might ignore them rather than risk another rejection. In addition to this, the perceived omission might well be remembered and stored in the 'Stroke Bank' for retaliation at a later date.

This same principle can be usefully applied to the socialization of knowledge through an organization. Imagine a new recruit who is motivated, focused and has a real talent for discovering new ideas. The first time the recruit comes up with an idea, it is discussed with a colleague and they decide to proceed and put the suggestion to the product review board. The next time nothing might come back from the colleague. Then there is every chance that the recruit might feel a sense of unease – possibly that the Knowledge Bank is too biased in one direction. As a result, the individual might take ideas straight to the review board and bypass the other person.

If this happens the socialization process is in danger of breaking down as people start to act in an insular and selfish way. Hence, knowledge that might have been shared, becomes rationed and held in personal squirrel stores. There it is retained until the individual sees a chance to share it with people who are prepared to reciprocate with ideas from their knowledge banks.

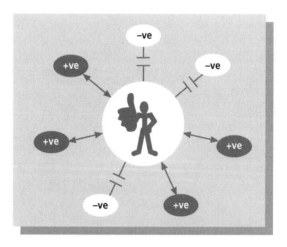

Figure 9.3

As a consequence we may construct a tacitly held map of individuals who are in debit and credit with regard to knowledge sharing as seen in Fig. 9.3. The net result is that invisible points of blockage can emerge in the social system, especially where we have a negative balance with more than one individual. If this happens, then these people can effectively be ostracized from the knowledge network. As a result they don't offer knowledge and are not consulted about ideas as they flow through the business.

Although this idea might appear to be conceptual and somewhat inconsequential, it takes on a degree of importance when considered in relation to the use of internal computer networks. The installation of a new intranet system will rely heavily on the knowledge accounts that we build. If you believe that you are doing all the contributing and other people are just extracting information, there is every chance that you might choose to socialize your knowledge using other, more traditional, processes. The end result is that a significant capital investment for the business can end up as a white elephant.

Communities of interest

Communities of interest are generally groups of people who meet informally to share ideas or learn from one another. They consist of people who carry out similar roles, share similar competencies, or have a shared outcome. The sales team that meets together every morning for coffee so that it can talk about the client accounts, or the football supporters that follow the same team. It may be that they have little in common but for this one key thing: they share an interest that they are keen to talk about.

The community's main process for learning is through the sharing of stories and personal anecdotes. To an outsider this approach might appear to be of little value, however, it can actually be more powerful than the traditional forms of teaching. We recount stories not just because the performance is enjoyable, but in order to influence other people's understanding of events and so illustrate their personal knowledge. They will often contain elements of humour, realism and words appropriate to the setting. This facilitates the general shifting of knowledge from one group to another without any work on the recipient's part.

One area where the storytelling process can take on a new form is in the generation and synthesis of new knowledge. In the case where different people recount their stories from opposite perspectives, they are able to develop a shared schema of the situation and so enlarge their personal understanding and the collective knowledge of the organization. Once this shared, collective story is understood by the various members, it becomes explicit knowledge that they can take away and enact within their own circles of influence.

"At the core of the twenty-first century company is the question of participation"

When considering stories as sharing tools, you should be wary of distortion. First of all, the subjective element of the story means that some degree of distortion will occur in the general message and meaning that is offered. Second, language is open to misunderstanding and misinterpretation, so that misrepresentation might occur in the translation process. However, as long as the basic underlying message remains core to the story any misinterpretation should be of an incidental nature.

Organizations are webs of participation. Change the patterns of participation and you change the organization. At the core of the twenty-first century company is the question of participation. At the heart of participation is the mind and spirit of the knowledge worker. Put simply, you cannot compel enthusiasm and commitment from knowledge workers. Only workers who choose to opt in – who voluntarily make a commitment to their colleagues – can create a winning company. When a company acknowledges the power of community and adopts elegantly minimal processes that allow communities to emerge, it is taking a giant step into the twenty-first century.[6]

At Xerox, for example, the goal of developing reusable software code seemed unattainable until a group of young engineers, working outside official channels, organized themselves under the banner of the Toolkit Working Group. These engineers weren't an official task force. They were an informal band of colleagues held together by friendships and loyalties forged during their intense collaboration on writing software for the company's 5090 copier line.

When the 5090 hit the market, it was time for this group to disband and work on new products, which meant reinventing much of the code they had already written. But they had a different agenda and decided to act on it. Beginning with virtually no official sanction and while still meeting new product obligations, the group pursued its reusable software vision and managed to do in three years what official task forces and project teams hadn't done in five.

Companies do much of their most important work through communities of interest – especially in the overlaps and alliances that bring disparate and conflicting communities together. Indeed, it is precisely in these overlaps that core competencies and social capital live. Most companies make the mistake of defining competencies as discrete technologies: patents, trade secrets, proprietary designs. But a real-world competence – a sustained capacity to outperform the competition – is built as much on implicit and tacit know-how and relationships as on tangible products and tools. You can't divorce competencies from the social fabric that supports them.

Diffuse questions

- How do you share your ideas with other people?

- How do you share your skills and behaviours with others?

- How do you share your emotions with others?

- Have you taken on-board someone else's ideas, skills or emotions recently – what happened and was the process effective?

- Can you describe how you explain complex or difficult things to others – what strategies do you use?

- Have you ever had a mentoree or coachee – how did you help them to take on-board some of your deeper capabilities?

- How do you build trust with another person so that they will share their knowledge with you?

- Are you prepared to share your knowledge with a competitor inside the organization?

- Do you ever use the idea of knowledge favours when exchanging knowledge with others?

- Are you a member of any communities of interest – do they increase your capacity to create a market value?

10

Knowledge delivery

The wise see knowledge and action as one.

Bhagvad-Gita

Ultimately, the acquisition of new knowledge must be done with a purpose and this purpose is to add value to the individual, team or organization. Once you have accrued certain knowledge assets, you are free (in theory) to create a market value, capitalize on this asset and so generate a payback. This payback might be financial, as with the monthly pay cheque; emotional in the gratitude received when the local charity is offered free advice; or physical in the break that people get on the annual holiday.

The reality is that very few delivery processes will draw upon just a single knowledge currency. Take any human activity and it will generally draw upon all three-knowledge currencies at both the explicit and tacit level. Trainers have to use their bodies to teach, their minds to map the learning process and their affections to engage the audience; musicians must use their hands to play their instruments, their heads to map the chord shapes and their emotions to add a personal interpretation.

The suggestion is not that you should try to separate the different knowledge components, but ideally understand how they integrate to create a market value. For any action where knowledge is being delivered, you might need to understand what currency is being used; what knowledge has a greater priority; and which of the three currencies (head, hand or heart) needs to be improved to enhance your market value.

Deliver matrix

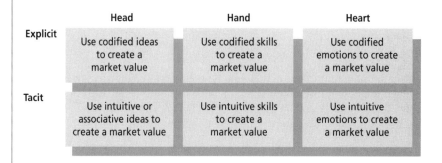

	Head	Hand	Heart
Explicit	Use codified ideas to create a market value	Use codified skills to create a market value	Use codified emotions to create a market value
Tacit	Use intuitive or associative ideas to create a market value	Use intuitive skills to create a market value	Use intuitive emotions to create a market value

Figure 10.1

Explicit head

In simple terms, this is the process you are following at the moment. In reading the words on this page you are the recipient of the explicit ideas that I wish to deliver to the world. This is a simple indication of the way we use our ideas, thoughts, mental models and schemata to create a market value in the world. Consider the teacher that offers children the theory of Pythagoras, the newsreader outlining the latest problems with the railways, or the child who offers to write someone's homework in exchange for a bag of sweets.

Explicit hand

Like the previous component, this one can be seen in the skills that a keynote presenter uses to engage and electrify the audience, or how the footballer scores a goal from the halfway line. The benefit of this component is the ability to measure both the process of delivery and the content. In most cases, explicit skills can be seen, measured, understood and replicated by others.

Explicit heart

This is less visible than the previous two, although in many ways it can offer greater value. The capability to deliver value in this area means that you have the ability to manage your own and others emotions effectively. You are able to outline your personal goals; ambitions, desires and values and more importantly work with others to understand theirs and how the two can be aligned.

Tacit head

This is a component that can be harder to understand and map in the K-Profile. Very often we will take actions or decisions without really understanding why or how we took them. This is because we have entrenched mental models that drive and guide how we operate in the world. I personally have deep and embedded beliefs about the way that I should treat other people. I might find it difficult to quickly explain or codify exactly what these beliefs are, but given time I would be able to. In the same way, look around any organization and there will be artefacts, processes and systems that indicate the tacit structure that underlies the rules and regulations of the business. In one company the MD might wish to have sight of all expense claims submitted by the sales teams, in another they might be signed off by the individual's line manager. This gives a strong indication of the tacit ideas that are being used by the MD. Whereas one believes in delegated responsibility, the other might take a more centralized approach.

Tacit hand

This is the way we naturally behave when presenting ourselves to the market. Think of the last presenter you experienced. Although many of the presentations skills might have been professionally honed by attending a training course, there will have been elements that were intuitively their own. The way the presenter talked, the design of the slides, or the facial expressions when faced with a difficult question are examples of tacit behaviour. These are things that we do quite intuitively when presenting ourselves to the market. We can change this tacit behaviour, but it will take time and we might have to work hard to sustain it. One classic example of someone who enhanced her market value by managing her tacit behaviour is Margaret Thatcher. In her early years as Prime Minister of Great Britain, she modified her image to the public by taking voice coaching lessons and dropping her voice by several tones. This was driven by the desire to soften her image and to give her a more authoritative stance when presenting.

Tacit heart

This can be quite a difficult component to deconstruct. Think about people who you value and like to spend time with. Now think about people who you value less highly and tend not to spend time with. The difference between these two groups might be driven by your tacit heart. Consider Peter who has just attended a managing effective relationship skills course and returned to work in the belief that he can now work with anyone. The problem is that once he tries to put the theory into action, he manages to use the techniques with people he likes and knows, but finds it difficult to use them with people he is less close to. This is because, underlying the explicit relationship skills that have been learnt on the course, he is still influenced by the deep emotional feelings that drive how he relates to other people. This is interesting because it is the one area that is rarely discussed in the workplace, but possibly has the most impact on how we manage the business. I have worked in companies that have been downsizing and seen people made redundant purely on the strength of senior managers negative tacit feelings about people they've worked with in the past. This is a powerful tool in the delivery armoury, but one that can cause problems if not understood and carefully managed.

The delivery stage of the framework is one of the most important of the five stages. You might be able to manage the discover, delay, dispose and diffuse stages impeccably, but unless these are focused on some form of market delivery, then it will all be to waste. This is why delivery is the point of interconnection – where personal knowledge becomes personal capital and capital that must be presented to the market in as attractive a way as possible.

In the next section I challenge you to think about the following:

● Can I place a market value on my personal capital?

● How do I balance the relationships with my employer and the market?

● Where do I position my personal capital in the market?

If you don't know or are not prepared to manage your value, then one of two things will occur. First, you might be selling yourself cheap and that means that someone else is taking your margin. Alternatively, you may be overpriced and one day a new downsizing exercise or competitor may come along and blow you out of the market. Only you will care about delivery value and only you will take the time to ensure it is placed in the right market to receive a fair return.

What's the delivery worth?

Owning capital is not a productive activity – Joan Robinson

Leigh Steinberg is one of the most powerful agents in sports and has been managing other people's market value for twenty-four years. He negotiated a contract for Ryan Leaf with the San Diego Chargers. At a certain point in the negotiation, the Chargers' general manager turned to Ryan and said, 'How can you ask for so much? You're going to be rich under any circumstances. All we're talking about is how rich you're going to be.'

Leigh agreed that there was some truth in that. But there's also truth in the fact that professional football generates tremendous revenue and players take enormous risks. He ended up getting Ryan Leaf $11.25 million as a signing bonus.[1] His goal was to balance up Ryan's market value with the income he received from the market. The reality is that in the knowledge era we no longer compete at the corporate or division level. Market competition will soon operate at the individual level, where each and every person must find and negotiate (or get someone else to negotiate) his or her value in the market.

More than ever, knowledge workers can see and feel the direct relationship between the work they do and the market value of their companies. A small team of programmers, armed with a great idea and a few workstations, can write a new software package that generates hundreds of millions of dollars of revenue. A small creative team can develop an advertising campaign so compelling that it puts its agency on the map – and leads to an enormous increase in billings. Not surprisingly, people with this much impact want to share in the value they create. They want a piece of the action. Knowledge workers realize that getting a 'salary' doesn't make sense for them. The value of what they contribute isn't based on the time they put in. A person who has a brilliant idea in the morning while he's shaving may be responsible for a breakthrough that vastly increases the value of the company. That person expects to be rewarded for those results.[2]

However, there is a deepening chasm that exists between the requirements of today's new economy and the business skills that will be essential to competing effectively in this revolutionary and evolving marketplace. One of the key differences will be between those who deliver time for income and those who deliver knowledge. The big difference between delivering these two factors is that time can be measured and monitored – knowledge is subjective and intangible, so the marketing and sales process is quite different.

Before you sell anything, you need to sell yourself. The primary power tool for that pitch is your K-Profile. Your K-Profile is you and as such it is in your interest to keep it up to date and focused on your desired market. Ask yourself: Are you adding something every 90 days? Have you shared the delivery components with future clients? And is it held in places where you can readily access and change the data?

The whole idea of personal marketing is introspection. You need the clearest possible view of your goals, both professional and personal. So start with a comprehensive personal inventory: What knowledge is contained within your K-Profile? How robust is your portfolio? What do you value most? Is it short-term gain or long-term security? Is it the ability to live or work in a certain geographic area? Is it the culture of your company or the attitudes of the people you work with? Is it a high degree of autonomy or an opportunity to be creative? Is it something as simple as the hours you work, the amount of vacation time you get, or the size and quality of your office? In this constellation of values, each factor may be important, but the question is, what is most important? Before you enter a negotiation with the market, you need to establish your priorities.[3]

The reality is that there is no one right set of delivery components that can be guaranteed to grow market value. People have spent years trying to find a valid, objective measure that can apply to all people, everybody in the same kind of job, or everybody in the same company. It's almost impossible: no two jobs are alike, no two companies are alike. The end result is that there is no one metric that everyone can agree on. Instead, it might be easier to use a definition like the one sometimes used for pornography: 'Nobody can tell you how to measure it, but everybody knows it when they see it'.[4] The challenge is for you to know your value and then help other people to see it.

‼ No two jobs are alike, no two companies are alike‼

After you've come to terms with the value of your knowledge, the next step is to understand your differentiator in the world. What are your unique skills and talents? Are you irreplaceable because of those skills and talents, or could anyone fill your slot? To answer these questions, you need to do some research into your own performance and there are all sorts of tools that you can use. There are internal and external documents that address the issue of employee value and sometimes you can get actual employee ratings. You can also get important information by talking and listening to other people: What is the market for your services outside your company? What are employees paid at other, comparable companies?[5]

Ultimately, there is no simple list of contact points that I can offer to define and measure your market value. As mentioned, your market value is dependent upon your content, context and motivation. If you want to map and measure your market value, then the first port of call is to hit the discover stage of the K-Profile and discover what market benchmark and guidelines are used to determine pay and market rates in your current or desired market sector.

Market thinking

For me, one of the most inexplicable observations in business life is the way that marketing experts can lead a company into new and rich markets, but at the same time totally mess up their personal careers. I know of so many people who have the qualifications and experience, who are able to analyze and predict business markets to an amazing degree, but when it comes to their next career move they make decisions that take them into blind alleys, low margin companies and industries that are about to fall flat. The core message here is that personal marketing is no different to business marketing – it just needs the appropriate desire and application. Ultimately, you must be in the position to at least match the customer's demands and where possible exceed and drive them.

Now, the intention of this section of the book is not to delve into the intricacies of market economics. The goal is for you to treat yourself as a business trading in the open market. If you already operate as a sole trader, then these principles will be second nature to you. However, the challenge here is for those people who don't operate in an open market and actually operate in a political market, i.e. working for someone else in a medium to large company.

The challenge is to understand the supply and demand equation and apply them in such a situation. In order to take this step you might need to rethink the underlying economic model that is applied in business. When a company recruits an employee, it generally does so on the economic model shown in Fig. 10.2. With this approach the employee is assumed to be owned by the company, as such the individual forgoes much to the risk associated with operating in a competitive and open market. However, employees also forgo much of the margin on their personal capital.

Now, this economic model made sense in a world where the ability to make a market relied on the ownership of land and capital, but does it make sense in a world where revenue is driven by access to the customer and the ability to offer an idea that people like? If you have personal capital that is valued by the market, why should you give such a large piece of your income away and act as a corporate slave? This is type one thinking, where you trade off income for the security of working for a large company and all the associated benefits. However, let us rethink this model. Twenty years ago such a notion was valid because there were secure jobs and companies could manage the market to ensure their longevity. Now, with the shift to the knowledge era, the whole notion of large company security is bunkum. There is no long-term security in a large company – so, if this is the case, why should you give away such a large chunk of your personal capital?

This takes us to type two thinking as shown in Fig. 10.3. With this way

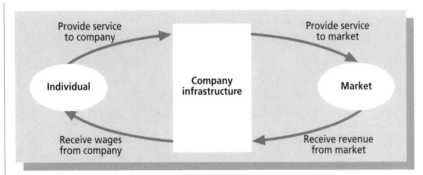

Figure 10.2
Type one thinking

of working, you take responsibility for your personal capital and treat the end customer as your market. You start to understand the value of your personal capital and think in a new way. Now you are generating the revenue from the market and you choose to give a percentage of your income to the company infrastructure as a reward for giving you access to the market.

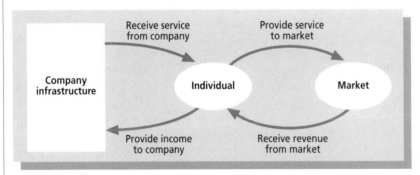

Figure 10.3
Type two thinking

By looking at the delivery stage from this perspective, you can start to understand the supply and demand profiles in more depth. No longer are you cushioned from the realities of life by the corporate machine – instead you view yourself and 'me.inc', with all the problems of brand development, market entry and financial control.

Once you are able to take this approach, then the K-Profile can help you to understand and define how the market values the different elements within your personal capital portfolio. Take each of the six elements in the delivery stage and start to consider how much the market values these elements. For the explicit head: What are my unique market propositions? Who are the competitors? and How much does the market value my ideas? For the explicit heart consider: What is the value of my network? Who buys repeat business from me? and How can I enhance my ability to manage relationships? For the tacit hand ask: What intuitive skills do I have that create value? Who values these? and Who else in the market is as good as me at doing these things?

Type two thinking is not undemanding and is certainly not easy for those of us who have been conditioned for twenty years or more into type one thinking. However, I would argue that, as the trappings associated with the knowledge era encroach more and more into how societies function, it will become the normal way of thinking. Unless you are able to think this way now, I believe that you will limit any chance to truly exploit the value of your personal capital. You also leave yourself at risk of being left high and dry the next time your employer decides to change its staffing policies.

● Market position

Once you have determined the worth of your personal capital, the next stage is to think about how you position yourself in the market. I tend to find that market position is driven by two primary factors: the extent to which I am able to differentiate my offerings and how much I charge. Although there are many other factors that contribute to the market mix, for a quick and dirty sense of where I should operate, these two hit the spot relatively quickly. We can use these two factors to develop the matrix shown in Fig. 10.4. This is a market position model that challenges you to think about where you sit at the moment and where you want to sit so as to fully exploit your personal capital.

The suggestion is that you can opt to sit in any one of the four boxes in the matrix, depending how much you and the market value your personal capital. The four options are as follows.

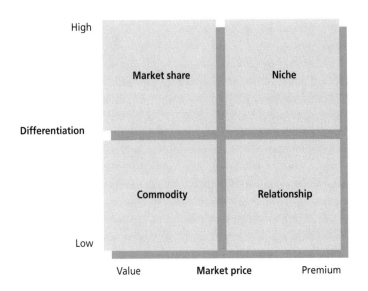

Figure 10.4
Market position
matrix

Commodity

If you operate in this area you operate in a market that will generally have low entry barriers, but with the trade off that it will not generate significant margins. The upside is that, with low start up costs, you have the flexibility to enter and withdraw from the market without taking a major risk. The downside is that it can be quite a battle, especially to maintain the low cost base that this type of market requires. Examples of roles in this type of market will be those jobs that might be found in most employment centres or job agencies. We can start to see increased interest in the area from the new portfolio worker. If someone wants to balance their work and personal life, they might choose to have two or more positions from this segment. The result is that they have a spread of income and the flexibility to shift and rotate jobs at will.

Market share

In this quadrant, your aim is to enter the market as a specialist but with a low price position. The upside of this type of approach is that it offers the chance to get your personal brand known quickly in the market and to recoup some early revenue back on your investment costs. The downside is that you incur a degree of risk. If your specialist area is based upon something that was costly to acquire and you cannot generate the appropriate returns, then you will run the risk of falling at the first hurdle. The other point to consider is what type of knowledge does your specialism rely on. If it is a tacit-based delivery, then it will be difficult for other people to copy or replicate the offering. However, if it is an explicit-based offering, the risk is that a competitor will take your ideas and then offer them at a discounted rate to yours. I have seen this approach being taken by a large number of web design companies that have surfaced with the growth of the Internet. As more and more people are gaining expertise in the field, so they are all trying to grow market share, which has resulted in pressure being placed on the day rate. If you operate in this field, the one question that you must ask is: What can I do to realize the appropriate gain for my personal capital and how do I shift into the premium pricing range of the market?

Relationship

One way to move into the premium pricing range is to spend more time on the softer aspects. Rather than trying to sell your products it can pay to sell you; to focus on the idea of developing relationships with your client base and only then move to a position where you sell your personal products. This is a classic marketing model and one that consultants exploit constantly. The upside is that it can help to lock in a long-term revenue stream and generate above average market return on your capital. The downside is that it can lead to over dependence and lock-in that can prove disastrous if the person moves on or you lose the relationships.

Niche

Finally, it is possible to generate a premium return by offering a product that is unique in the marketplace. The benefit is that your ability to differentiate at a personal level can help build long-term revenue streams that are built around you rather than your employer. The downside is that markets can be fickle and change overnight. What was yesterday's busting product is often to be found in the bargain bin a week later. So, if you follow this strategy, it is wise to ensure that you have contingency plans or products that you can call on if the market changes.

The whole point with this four-market position not to infer what the right market entry point is, rather it is to challenge you to think about your personal capital in detail and position each element within the four boxes. If you are comfortable with the upside and risk profiles then fine, if not then you need to think carefully about how you position your delivery stage both now and in the future.

Deliver questions

- To what extent do you effectively use all your knowledge to create a market value?

- What is more important – your explicit or your tacit value in the market?

- What is your market value?

- How do you use your head currency to create a value in the market?

- How do you sell your skills?

- To what extent do your emotions amplify or diminish the value of your personal capital?

- Can you describe your brand value in a few words to another person?

- What knowledge will you need in one, three and five years' time?

- What risks will you take to realize your market value?

- To what extent do you negotiate your worth in the market?

- How much do your customers value what you offer over and above your competitors?

- What new knowledge do you plan to acquire in the future?

- What value will it have?

11

Building a K-Profile

You can do anything you think you can. This knowledge is literally the gift of the gods, for through it you can solve every human problem. It should make of you an incurable optimist. It is the open door.

Robert Collier

The three areas of knowledge: stock, flow and currency can be synthesized to produce a knowledge map or K-Profile. This is a total picture of the knowledge that an individual has to manage in order to create a market value. The schematic map consists of ten knowledge areas, each of which indicates a particular action that is being taken about a form of explicit or tacit knowledge as seen in Fig. 11.1.

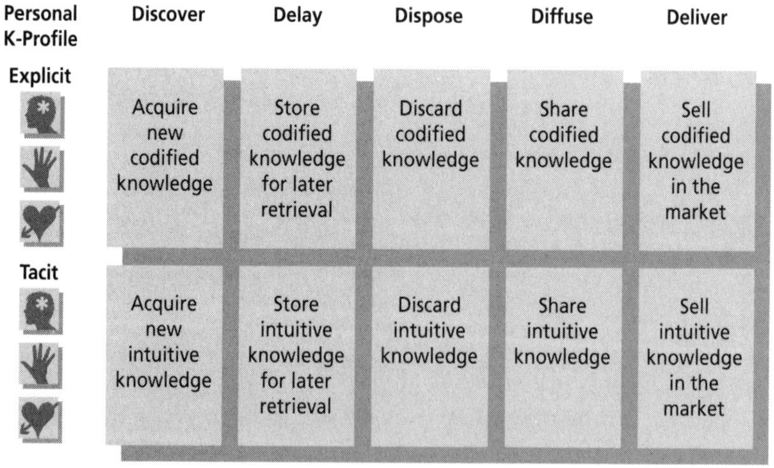

Personal K-Profile	Discover	Delay	Dispose	Diffuse	Deliver
Explicit	Acquire new codified knowledge	Store codified knowledge for later retrieval	Discard codified knowledge	Share codified knowledge	Sell codified knowledge in the market
Tacit	Acquire new intuitive knowledge	Store intuitive knowledge for later retrieval	Discard intuitive knowledge	Share intuitive knowledge	Sell intuitive knowledge in the market

Figure 11.1
K-Profile

At any moment in time, an individual might undertake one or more of the actions listed in Fig. 11.1. So the student who is attending an evening class will primarily discover new explicit ideas, but might also be influenced, at a tacit heart level, by the passion of the lecturer. In another example, the football coach who is training a group of schoolchildren will be operating at the explicit behaviour level, but with some implicit ideas included when he describes how the skills fit into a range of tactical strategies. Finally, the manager who has just been recruited spends time with a more experienced customer service supervisor. Although the goal is for him or her to gain a deeper understanding of the internal processes used to deal with the customer (discover, head, explicit), the deeper idea is for him or her to gain a sense of emotional alignment with the problems the front-line staff face (discover, tacit, heart).

Building a K-Profile

In building your K-Profile, the objective is quite simple: to have each component within the profile completed, with data that is current, of significant quality and manageable. The K-Profile build can in some cases be quite difficult and in others relatively easy. This will depend on the following factors.

- Whether you are completing the K-Profile on your own, or will be able to elicit the help of a colleague or professional facilitator.
- Your level of understanding about knowledge management as a broad process.
- The extent to which you have previously mapped your personal competencies.
- Whether the decision to go through the process is your own or you have been pushed into the process as part of a larger programme.
- Whether you are completing the profile for your eyes only, or to share with other people.
- Whether you intend to use the tool on an ongoing basis, or to provide a profile snapshot.
- The period over which the K-Profile will be built. Since knowledge is

subjective in nature, your view of its construction and worth can change depending upon your feelings and the environment.

In many cases it can help to use your experience of learning about the K-Profile as the first element to include in the system. Consider, how are you learning about it (discover, explicit or tacit); Are you storing it in your memory or writing it down (delay, hard or soft)?; Have you had to let go of any preconceptions about knowledge management to accept the ideas (disposal)?; Who will you tell about your experience (diffuse); and, at this moment in time, what value do you see in the model (deliver)?

Answers to these questions will give you an initial set of data to put in the component boxes. Once you have mapped your first knowledge area, think about another important knowledge element that you currently use and ask yourself the same questions. After a while you will see the profile appear in front of your eyes with hardly any effort.

The whole idea is that the K-Profile is a personal record and as such will be dynamic in nature and dependent upon where we are at any moment in time. Like a company balance sheet, it can only represent your knowledge profile at one unique moment in time. A second after you have completed the current version, you might find an article that helps you to think about a new market offering. The trick is not to see this as a problem, but more as an opportunity. Once you start to understand the dynamics of the K-Profile, you will develop a clearer appreciation of your learning style.

> **"** Once you start to understand the dynamics of the K-Profile, you will develop a clearer appreciation of your learning style **"**

● Question types

Within the K-Profile, there are three dimensions that need to be addressed and the questions used to pull off the component data must reflect these aspects. They are:

- questions to determine whether the knowledge is stored in tacit or explicit form;
- questions to understand what currency is used to engage and create value in the market;

- questions to understand the way you process knowledge as it flows through the system.

Clearly it is impossible to develop a set of standard formulae or questions that can be used to build your personal K-Profile. Although I cannot offer a series of panacea questions that will extract your knowledge base, it is possible to indicate the type of approach that can be used for each of the core areas in the K-Profile.

Explicit

Of the two stock question sets, this area is generally the easiest. In mapping the explicit area you will simply indicate what you can explain to other people. This is often referred to as declarative knowledge in that it is something that you can assert or explain to another person. Hence you might ask yourself: What do I know? What skills do I have? or How do I feel about a certain topic or person? The fact that you can simply and quickly explain certain things suggests that they might fall into the explicit domain.

Tacit

Any question you ask will generally be based around a procedure or 'how to' or 'why do you'. So the explicit question might consider what you know, but the tacit element is concerned with how you know that or why you use that knowledge. One of the ways to elicit this type of knowledge is by asking 'if' and 'then' questions. If Z happens, how do I behave? and Why do I take that action? If you then funnel down by asking the why question several times, then you will be homing in on the tacit element.

One simple guide is that tacit knowledge is often heuristic in form in that it is a personal rule of thumb used to manage your world.

Head

At this stage questions are used to understand how you think about certain topics. They might be: What mental model do I have that other people value? How do I plan certain actions? What techniques do I use to manage a situation? Why do I take certain actions in one situation and different actions in another? One of the problems at this stage can be having consciousness about your unconsciousness. In the same way that fish are the last ones to see the water, understanding how we see the world can be difficult. We all use filters or schematic barriers that bend and shape how we see and interact with the world. So, although the first stage in understanding the head area might be to look at your CV to reflect on what you know, it might be useful to get feedback from friends or colleagues who can offer their perspective on what they think you know.

Hand

In mapping our behaviour, we are trying to understand our skills and physical capabilities. This might be the ability to operate a piece of machinery, lead a class of rebellious children, or use techniques to close a large sale. The questions are largely around what I do rather than why or how I do it. Of the three areas in the currency section, this one is probably the easiest area from which to gather rich data. Your skills might be written down already in your CV and can in many cases be simply translated directly into the K-Profile.

Heart

It can be quite difficult to develop reflective questions that will extract this information. This is about your inter and intra personal skills, i.e. how you deal with yourself and others. The questions you might ask are: How do I feel about a certain person? and What impact does this have on my market value? Can I change how I feel about someone? or How do I manage relationships with my colleagues?

Discover

Questions around the five flow stages are often simpler since they have a more tangible basis. The questions might be: How do I acquire new knowledge? What information sources do I have? How do I prioritize the information I internalize and use? and How do I ascribe value to incoming data?

Delay

With this stage, one of the additional areas to consider is whether you store information in a fixed, firm or fluid system. To what extent is knowledge stored within the short- and long-term memory systems and at what point is it transferred to some form of hard storage (e.g. processes, procedures or systems).

Dispose

Of the five stages in the flow section, these questions might be the hardest. The process of unlearning is something that is rarely taught, considered or generally discussed as part of the knowledge process. To understand how you unlearn it might be simplest to think about what you have forgotten. Look back over a diary and think back to previous projects. Think about the techniques, knowledge and ideas you used at those points and consider whether that approach or knowledge is still valid. If not, how did you let go and what process can you use to enhance you ability to let go of the past?

Diffuse

Sharing questions are relatively easy to deal with. Ask yourself who you talk with about important subjects. Consider who you don't talk with. What is the difference? And what value of information do you offer to others? and, possibly, Do you look for reward for sharing?

Deliver

Finally, the most crucial question of all: How do you create value in the market? Although the basic idea is quite simple, this can be a difficult one to deal with. We are often so conditioned to think of reward in terms of hours performed or the job title we hold, that developing an appreciation of our market value can be difficult. The question here might be around the number of repeat requests you get for your services; what people ask from you; your most valuable personal asset; or the most important areas in your personal objectives. The problem with this stage is that it is so content and context dependent that I could reel off a hundred questions, none of which might have any personal relevance for you. The problem here is a catch-22 issue. Until you understand how to understand your market value, how do you know what questions to ask yourself? Often the only way to break this loop is to write something down and share it with other people. Take a stab at your three core value areas – think about what other people value in you – and then share it with colleagues. Their feedback will help you to understand how the market might value your knowledge.

Interestingly, by going through such a process you can gauge how far out your judgement is in determining value.

The goal with any knowledge elicitation process is not to take the big bang approach. Don't try to get everything down with all the detail. Just go for the high level stuff with maybe three or four knowledge chunks in each component.

> **"** *The goal with any knowledge elicitation process is not to take the big bang approach* **"**

K-Profile data

When you start to think about questions needed to build a K-Profile, one of the points of confusion can be about the type of data to go in each area. Although the end data will be dependent upon how you choose to use the K-Profile, ultimately there can be as many data descriptions as you care to think of.

First, is it action-based knowledge and something that is described though the use of a verb? Alternatively, are you describing a stock element that is something static that exists in asset form and can be described using a noun? Second, is the knowledge being deployed in a positive way to enhance your personal value? Alternatively, is it a being deployed in a negative way that detracts from the personal value you aspire to build? By a combination of these two ranges we can develop the matrix shown in Fig. 11.2.

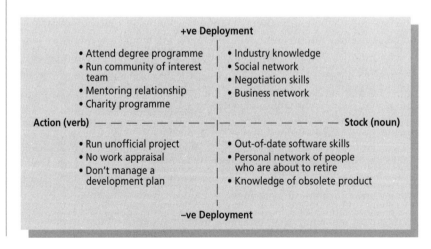

Figure 11.2
K-Profile content

It is not necessary to labour over the difference between the verb and noun description, because, in the vast majority of cases, a verb statement should result in a stock item being held as personal capital. However, it does make a difference if the tool is being used for a specific purpose or if someone else will use it.

The third factor might be to show if it is current or anticipated knowledge. If the K-Profile is being built as a here and now picture, then all of the components will show stock or actions that are in place. However, if it is being used as a coaching tool, it might be that all or some of the knowledge is future-based.

This can be a dynamic, complex and difficult process to undertake. It will be a challenge in that it might be asking you to think in a new way; manage your life differently; and at the end of the day take a much more reflective view of the world. So often we try to create value by being 'out there' and selling ourselves. The assertion with this model is that before you can be 'out there' selling yourself, you have to look inwards to understand your real commercial viability. Only once you can be honest with yourself and build a truly representative K-Profile can you hope to create long lasting market value.

K-Profile questions

Your K-Profile will be driven by your goals and will, therefore, draw upon questions and frameworks that fit your view of the world. However, the questions in the table below will help to start the first stage of the build process.

Discover

Explicit

- *Stock* What new ideas have you acquired in the past twenty-four hours? How will they be used?

- *Flow* How do you decide what knowledge to acquire or ignore?

- How do you create new ideas?

- *Future* What do you need to do to improve how you acquire new knowledge?

- *Stock* What new skills have you acquired in the past twenty-eight hours?

- *Flow* What are the channels by which you acquire new skills?

- *Future* How can you enhance your ability to gain new skills and competencies?

- *Stock* What new motivation have you acquired recently or what new relationships have you forged?

- *Flow* How do you decide who to build relationships with and what goals to focus on?

- *Future* Are there any better ways to build more effective relationships?

Tacit

- *Stock* What filters drive how you view the world and acquire new knowledge?

- *Flow* How do you manage your filters to ensure that valuable knowledge is not excluded?

- *Future* What mental model would you like to have that drives how you acquire new ideas?

- *Stock* What would your friends say is your greatest ability when acquiring new skills?

- *Flow* Do you absorb new skills through practice, experience and perseverance, or can you take them on board with little training?

- *Future* How could you acquire new expertise?

- *Stock* Who do you naturally work with when acquiring new knowledge? Why? Who do you intuitively choose not to work with? Why? What is the difference between the two relationships?

- *Flow* When in a new situation, what intuitive steps do you take to forge new relationships? Why?

- What works? Why? What doesn't work? Why?

- How do you motivate yourself to learn?

- What would other people say is your greatest motivation to learn and acquire knowledge?

- *Future* How would you like to build effective relationships in the future?

Delay

Explicit

- *Stock* Where are your ideas and thoughts stored? (Fixed, firm or fluid)

- *Flow* Do you understand how you store and delay knowledge that is not currently in use?

- How do you ensure that ideas shift from short-term to long-term memory?

- How do you decide where to store the ideas?

- *Future* How do I need to store them in the future?

- *Stock* What skills do you have that are not being used in the market?

- *Flow* How have you decided that they should be in storage and not used to create market value?

- *Future* What future skills do you need to have in store ready to use?

- *Stock* Who do you have bankable relationships with that you can call on?

- What inner resources or plans do you have for yourself?

- How do your emotions impact upon your ability to hold and store knowledge?

- *Flow* How do you decide when to use the relationships?

- *Future* What emotional strengths and relationships will you need in the future?

Tacit

- *Stock* What historic ideas and beliefs guide how you think today?

- Do your short- and long-term memories get biased by your personal filters?

- *Flow* How do you choose what stored beliefs to accept as true?

- *Future* What ideas do you want to have in store to guide how you think?

- *Stock* To what extent do people ask for your help in areas that you might consider yourself as weak?

- *Flow* How do you choose when to give this help?

- *Future* What deep behaviours do you need to call upon in the future?

- *Stock* What would other people say are your emotional strengths?

- What people do you call upon when you have a problem?

- *Flow* How do you decide what people to work with when under pressure?

- *Future* What emotional stock will you need in the future to create your desired market value?

Dispose

Explicit

- *Stock* When was the last time you realized that you were wrong about something?

- *Flow* What process did you go through to change your mind?

- How adverse are you to change and letting go of the past?

- *Future* Can you think of ways that will help you to let go of redundant ideas in the future?

- *Stock* What was the last behaviour you changed because you realized that old way was not appropriate?

- *Flow* How difficult was it to change?

- *Future* What skills, capabilities or behaviours do you think you might have to lose in the future?

- *Stock* Can you think of a situation where you have overcome an emotional or motivational blockage?

- *Flow* How did you achieve it?

- *Future* What emotional blockages will you have to lose in the future?

Tacit

- *Stock* What deep beliefs have you changed recently?

- *Flow* How did you change them?

- *Future* What future emotions will you have to modify to improve your effectiveness?

- *Stock* If you asked a colleague, how would he or she say you have changed recently, in what way have you changed your behaviour?

- *Flow* What caused that to happen?

- *Future* What entrenched behaviours will you have to modify in the future?

- *Stock* How would other people describe changes in your emotional state or relationship with them over recent months?

- *Flow* Why did you change?

- To what extent do your emotions impact upon your ability to let go of the past?

- *Future* What deep emotional changes will you have to instigate over the coming months?

Diffuse

Explicit

- *Stock* What is your current formal or informal social network where you share ideas?

- *Flow* How do you decide whom to share the ideas with?

- *Future* What future networks do you need to join or cultivate?

- *Stock* Where do you share skills and behaviours with other people?

- *Flow* How do you decide what skills to share or receive from colleagues?

- *Future* What new skills do you need to acquire from colleagues?

- *Stock* Who are your closest colleagues that you share you feelings with?

- Who are the people that you are not happy to share your feelings with?

- *Flow* Why do you share with one group and not the other?

- *Future* Who do you think you might get close to in the future?

Tacit

- *Stock* What would other people say about your ability to work in a network and share ideas?

- *Flow* Why would they say that?

- Can you reject ideas from colleagues that you don't agree with or do they still have an influence on your thoughts?

- *Future* What would you like them to say in the future?

- *Stock* What would colleagues say are the skills you have that they would like to acquire?

- *Flow* How do you think you might share the skills with them?

- *Future* What skills would you like to acquire through association with colleagues in the future?

- *Stock* What do other people value about your emotional capability when working in a group?

- *Flow* What is it about that capability that they might admire?

- *Future* If you were to take yourself forward six months, what new emotional capabilities would you like to share with colleagues?

Deliver

Explicit

- *Stock* What are your primary ideas and thoughts that create a market value?

- *Flow* How do you decide which ones to use at any moment in time?

- *Future* What future ideas are required by the market?

- What actions do you have in the discover stage to acquire these?

- *Stock* What are your skills and behaviours that are used in the market?

- *Flow* How do you decide which skills are of most value?

- How do you keep the skills up to date and marketable?

- *Future* What future skills do you need to acquire to maintain or enhance your market value?

- *Stock* How motivated are you to achieve your goals?

- Who are the people who value you most?

- *Flow* How do you maintain your motivation?

- How do you maintain your relationships in the market?

- *Future* What future goals do you need to generate?

- What future relationships do you need to build?

Tacit

- *Stock* What would others say are your great ideas and why?

- What filters do you use to take your ideas to market?

- *Flow* How do you reflect on and understand which ideas drive how you sell yourself and your products?

- *Future* If you moved forward one year, what ideas would be valued by the market?

- *Stock* What is it about your behaviour that others most value and why?

- *Flow* What are you doing to manage and enhance this behaviour?

- *Future* What skills would you like others to value in you in the future?

- *Stock* How would others value your relationships with them and why?

- How would other people describe your ability to motivate yourself?

- *Flow* How do you create this emotional value?

- *Future* What future emotional value would you like others to describe about you?

Look before you leap

The first time you try to complete the K-Profile it might feel difficult for a number of reasons, first is the fact that we are not really taught how to think about thinking. As a society we generally focus on the input or output stage of learning and the process in-between is left to happenstance. Second, it can seem daunting to have to think about so many different elements and pull them all together into a single entity. Finally, the tendency can be to jump in and fill out the easy areas and then get bored or put the process aside when you reach some of the harder questions.

One of the ways to avoid some of these problems is to sit down and think through the process of mapping your personal capital before you even pick up a pen to fill out the boxes. Just take a while and go through the following questions. In pre-thinking the process you will ensure that you are able to complete a K-Profile that is robust and adds real personal value.

Why am I doing this?

- Who is the K-Profile for? Are you building it for yourself, or are you helping someone else to build their profile?

- What is the desired outcome or purpose? Is it to be used as: a stock system to understand knowledge that exists; a flow system to understand how the knowledge is managed; a decision support system to help define what knowledge needs to be acquired; a personal log to support a development programme.

- What decisions do you want to make? Is the goal to change how you manage your knowledge, or is the goal to use knowledge to change other things in your life? Will any changes to the knowledge management process be under your control or will other people be involved (budget sign-off, etc)?

- Challenge how honest you (or the other) person will be in building the K-Profile. Are you really prepared to expose all your assets and liabilities, or is it simply a corporate exercise to 'map' the espoused competencies?

Where am I now?

- Consider what type of data you want to include in the K-Profile. From this, define where the data will come from. Is it from: your CV; feedback from colleagues or clients; internal reflection; company appraisals; previous competency mapping exercises; or through a personal diary system, where you monitor your knowledge processes over a typical week? Whatever the source, you need to be clear as to its currency, accessibility and legitimacy before you start the build process.

- Be clear on what problems might be encountered in building the matrix. Do you have time set aside and will there be professional support?

- What shadow data impacts on the K-Profile that you are prepared to include in the matrix. If you are unable or unwilling to include more sensitive data because others will see the K-Profile, then can you record it elsewhere for your eyes only?

- Can you get feedback from others on what knowledge chunks they believe should be included? This is one of the best ways to extract and understand some of your deeper tacit knowledge – see the world as others see you and I guarantee that you will be surprised, shocked and enlightened.

Create the K-Profile

- If this is a first time construction, then take a divergent approach and include as many knowledge areas as you can in the matrix. Take time to brainstorm and randomize all the possible knowledge chunks that might be included. Try to stretch yourself to really think about all the different roles and functions you perform where a market value is created. Only discard chunks once you are sure that they don't apply.

- If you find it difficult to break your life into market roles, then sit down and draw a rough storyboard of things you do each day. Draw a series of pictures that show what you do at different times. Once you have the rough pictures, look at them and consider what currencies are being used; are you using explicit or tacit knowledge and what knowledge stage is being used (Discover, Delay, etc)?

- If you are revising an existing K-Profile, take time to look at the whole picture and try to create a sense of balance across the matrix. Do you have a dominant area, where all of your effort is focused and should you be applying more effort in another stage, stock or currency area?

- The acquisition and delivery of knowledge is always underpinned by effort and energy. Even thinking about an idea means that you are allocating brain energy to a particular task as opposed to some other idea. Try to understand where this energy comes from and how it might be applied. Can you find other sources of personal energy, can other people help you when managing a particular knowledge component; or should you divert energy from other areas.

Measure the success

- As part of the build process, you might consider how you know what you know and how you will know when to get to the next stage. The problem with most personal development systems is that they elicit grandiose schemes and goals, but might not define how the transformation is to be measured. If you include data in the K-Profile that indicates what knowledge stock you have, be sure that you truly have the asset in place and that it is not clouded by your subjective bias.

- One point to consider is what type of measures you are using. Are they quantitative in that you are specifying how many assets you have, what rating you have attained for a certain skill, or what mark you aspire to in a future exam. The alternative measurement approach might be to use a qualitative process. Can you measure your current or planned knowledge in terms of how it feels, to you or others?

Make it last

- When you build the K-Profile with planned changes, it is important to consider how you will ensure that acquired knowledge will last. So often we make promises to others and ourselves about things we will do, feel or think in the future, but ultimately fail to deliver the goods. If the K-Profile is to help facilitate a change that will continue, it is important to consider what you can do now to make the acquisition or change process last. If you are about to embark on a new course, what can you do to ensure that you will see it through to the end? If you acquire a new set of skills, how can you make sure that you will not drift back to the old behaviour patterns? and If you have improved your relationship with a team member, what can you do to guarantee that the relationship will last?

- One of the ways to ensure that any planned changes will stick is to make sure you refresh and review the K-Profile on a regular basis. It is a rare person who does not learn something, however small, every day. Use of a constant refresh process will help you to keep the K-Profile constant, relevant and manageable.

This framework should be seen as a guiding hand not a prescriptive road map. You can only follow a build path that fits the content of the knowledge and the context in which you are building the K-Profile. However, whatever process you follow, I suggest that you scan some of the ideas in this framework, as they will be applicable to most, if not all, cases where a K-Build is taking place.

12

Reference K-Profiles

Knowledge is a deadly friend when no-one sets the rules.
The fate of all mankind, I see, is in the hands of fools.

King Crimson

One of the benefits of the K-Profile is that it can allow you to look at the knowledge flow process and start to understand what common knowledge management styles are used. Although this might lead to the accusation of stereotyping people and roles, it does help individuals and teams to make sense of the K-Profile.

The K-Profile will help you shift your knowledge management processes from tacit to explicit – so the definition of typical profiles can help you make sense of the model and its application. The intention is not for you to say 'I am this or that profile', but to understand that in certain situations you might behave in a certain way and to know how you might modify or improve that behaviour.

The profiles shown in this section have been built around the three primary filters listed below.

- **Acquire** indicates the source of the knowledge. Is it within a closed domain, for example within the person or team? Alternatively, is the data being acquired from outside the boundary the individual operates within?

- **Application** indicates whether the knowledge is being used to deliver results now, or is being used to create value in the future.

- **Age** specifies whether the data already exists and has simply been borrowed or extracted from an existing source, or if it is new to the individual or team.

Although I have identified six different profiles below, please don't assume that these are 'the' profiles. As mentioned already, the goal is not to define stereotypical profiles, it is simply a tool to help you understand how to manage knowledge in different situations. If you get the time, make some up for yourself. If you get more time, send them to me and I can publish them on the website (www.WizOz.co.uk).

One of the interesting things about the profiles is the spin that can be applied. For example, the broker profile is focused on the management and control of external data as it comes into the domain, uses existing information and deals in the present. As a broker the role is to create market value through the management and exploitation of existing knowledge. Now this might be seen as the upside profile, where this is a role that is typically valued within an organization. However, you can also spin this profile another way, to reflect that the same attributes might be found in the typical gatekeeper or someone who blocks the transfer of information within an organization.

For each of the six profiles, I have outlined the primary attributes that can be found in the upside role, but have also tried to consider what might be found in the downside. However, any ideas offered in the profile description are obviously filtered through my perspective of what is up and down. My guess is that you will disagree with some of the ideas and if you don't, then you should look again and find something to disagree with. The whole bedrock that underpins the knowledge model is grounded in the idea that knowledge is a subjective orientation – as such, any descriptor that tries to apply a good or bad side to the management of knowledge will be a subjective view and open to criticisms.

Apprentice / *Amateur*

Acquire	Application	Age
Internal	Future	Existing

Figure 12.1

Upside – Apprentice

The apprentice process might be defined as training in an art, trade or craft, under a legal agreement defining the relationship between master and learner and the duration and conditions of the relationship.

From the earliest times, in Egypt and Babylon, training in craft skills was organized to maintain craftsmen in adequate numbers. The laws of Hammurabi of Babylon, which date from the 18th century BC, required artisans to teach their crafts to the young. In some ancient societies, Rome for example, many craftsmen were slaves, but in the later years of the Roman Empire, craftsmen began to organize themselves into *collegia* to maintain the standards of their trades.

By the thirteenth century a similar practice reappeared in Western Europe with the emergence of the craft guilds, which supervised quality and methods of production and regulated conditions of employment for each occupational group in a town. The guilds were controlled by the master craftsmen and the recruit entered after a period of training as an apprentice, commonly lasting seven years. It was a system suited to domestic industry. The master operated on his own premises, where his assistants resided as well as worked. An artificial family relationship was thus created, with the articles of apprenticeship taking the place of kinship.

The notion of individual training extended beyond the craft guilds in the Middle Ages. The university accepted the same principle with its master's degree and the religious orders insisted on the newcomers passing through a novitiate. In medicine, the guild system applied to the surgeon, who also performed the function of barber and was regarded as a craftsman, with less prestige than the physician. The lawyer served an apprenticeship by working in close association with a master of the profession. This has persisted in England, with the articles of clerkship that bind pupils to a solicitor or barrister, but in the United States and in most European countries, the law degree is now the main avenue to the profession.[1]

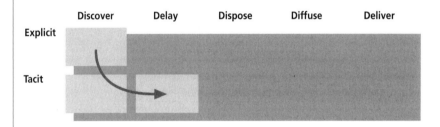

Figure 12.2
Apprentice profile

The possible profile for this type of knowledge role can be seen in Fig. 12.2. The core assumptions used to build the model are as follows.

● The discovery process is focused on the explicit and tacit components, although much of the primary focus should be on the tacit intake of information.

● The objective is for this to become embedded into the learner's deep, long-term memory.

● Much of the embedded knowledge must be at a tacit level.

The (general) assumption is that delivery is not a core part of the apprentice process. Although some market trade might occur, this is still only to reinforce the learning and transference to long-term memory.

● Downside – Amateur

This is not in any way meant to be derogatory to the amateur roles you have in your life. In this sense it draws upon the dictionary definition of an amateur as one who engages in a pursuit as a pastime rather than as a profession.[2] This falls in line with the view that someone who spends too long in the discovery and delay stage is not serious about creating personal market value by using his or her acquired knowledge and is more interested in the process of learning than in using the knowledge to create a market value.

This might be seen to occur when someone is so focused on the discovery stage that they never actually get to exploit the true market value of the knowledge they have acquired. I have seen people who get so entrenched with the idea of learning that they fail to realize that the point of learning is not learning itself – it is about creating market value that will reap reward from the learning process.

This potential problem can be seen in the growth of the slogan 'lifelong learning'. Clearly this is a positive step for any government to foster. However, one slight concern is that it places the emphasis on learning rather than the delivery of this learning. Consider the UK statement

> *Learning is the key to prosperity – for each of us as individuals, as well as for the nation as a whole. Investment in human capital will be the foundation of success in the knowledge-based global economy of the twenty-first century. This Green Paper sets out for consultation how learning throughout life will build human capital by encouraging the acquisition of knowledge and skills and emphasizing creativity and imagination. The fostering of an enquiring mind and the love of learning are essential to our future success.*[3]

The whole emphasis in this passage from the green paper is on the discovery stage of the knowledge profile; there is little that highlights how you can transfer this to the delivery stage.

The intention is not to criticize anyone or any agency involved in the Lifelong Learning initiative, simply to stress that learning without a knowledge management process can be a limiting activity. If you have spent a valuable chunk of time acquiring new knowledge, then it is important to ensure that this gets translated into market value and does not waste away as the world moves on around you.

● Broker / *Blocker*

Figure 12.3

Source	Application	Age
External	Now	Existing

● Upside – Broker

Brokers are people who use their embedded knowledge to identify opportunities to resell other people's knowledge and expertise. They act as an intermediary in a sale or other business transaction between two parties. They neither possess the goods sold nor receive the goods procured; they take no market risks and transfer no title to goods or to anything else. They earn commission, or brokerage, when the contract of sale has been made, regardless of whether the contract is satisfactorily executed.

Brokers are most useful in establishing trade connections in those large industries where a great many relatively small producers (e.g. farmers) compete for a wide market. They operate in strategic cities and keep in active touch with the trade needs of their localities and with one another. They are important in determining prices, routing goods and guiding production and in those functions play a part similar to that of the highly organized exchanges. Brokers also negotiate trades in property not directly affecting production, as for instance stockbrokers and real estate brokers.

Brokers can be found within an organization, but are not normally referred to as such. Consider the role played by internal change agents, professional service teams or internal purchasers. They act on behalf of the business, but do not own the inflows or outflows of goods or products. Their role is to ensure that customers facing business units have the correct supply of products to ensure that customer service is managed.

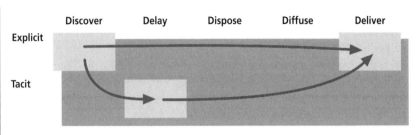

Figure 12.4
Broker profile

The key elements in the broker profile can be described as follows.

- In the majority of cases the discovery process will be explicit rather than tacit. The broker is driven by a need to be aware of the changing dynamics in the market.

- Decisions about what information can be brokered profitably are likely to be driven by a deep tacit understanding of what works in the market. The whole market value is driven by a deep and intuitive appreciation of what will sell in the market.

- This knowledge will generally be transferred directly to the delivery stage untouched.

One aspect of the broker role is that it can be a powerful agent for change as brokers provide linkage and fluidity across a dispersed social system. This can include teachers, consultants and newspaper journalists. All of these change agents provide a communication link between a resource system of some kind and a client system at the other end. In many cases the change agent might have expertise around the message being processed, but often it might only be a superficial understanding – sufficient to understand who needs the information and why.

Downside – Blocker

On the morning of 21 December 1970, Elvis Presley personally delivered a letter to the northwest gate of the White House. Written on American Airlines stationery, the five-page letter requested a meeting with President Nixon. Presley intended to present the President with a gift of a World War II pistol and obtain for himself the credentials of a federal agent.

```
Dear Mr. President.

First, I would like to introduce myself. I am Elvis
Presley and admire you and have great respect for your
office. I talked to Vice President Agnew in Palm Springs
three weeks ago and expressed my concern for our country.
The drug culture, the hippie elements, the SDS, Black
Panthers, etc. do NOT consider me as their enemy or as
they call it The Establishment. I call it America and
I love it. Sir, I can and will be of any service that
I can to help The Country out. I have no concern or
Motives other than helping the country out.

Respectfully,
Elvis Presley
```

Figure 12.5

President Nixon's appointments secretary suggested in a memo that Presley might be just the person for Mr Nixon to speak with, if he was interested in meeting 'some bright young people' outside the government. Next to this comment, H. R. Haldeman, the President's chief of staff, scrawled in pen 'You must be kidding.'

Bob Haldeman was best known for his role in the cover-up of the Richard M. Nixon administration's involvement in the 1972 break-in at the Democratic Party's National Committee headquarters in the Watergate complex in Washington, D.C. Haldeman served as campaign manager for Nixon's successful 1968 presidential campaign and became White House chief of staff when Nixon took office. He was extremely powerful in that position and was often referred to as 'the keeper of the gate' because of his ruthlessness in limiting access to the President. Hence one of his primary roles could be seen as someone who would block the flow of any information to the President that would limit his effectiveness or personal market value.

The process of information management is underpinned by the idea of effective channel management. The added value from the gatekeeper role is not in the ability to manipulate or change the content or form of the information; rather it is to ensure that those people who can add value receive the information in an appropriate and timely fashion. By doing this, they actually have a significant impact on the knowledge system, primarily because they act as attenuators and amplifiers.

The ability to manage the flow of information through the system is often an overlooked capability within the knowledge system. This ability is often seen in the guise of opinion formers or change agents, people who have the power to control who sees what and when. Any organization should be acutely aware of the location of these opinion formers and understand the potential that they have to amplify or attenuate ideas and knowledge. Consider the implication of a person who sits in a gatekeeper position within the business.

"The ability to manage the flow of information through the system is often an overlooked capability within the knowledge system"

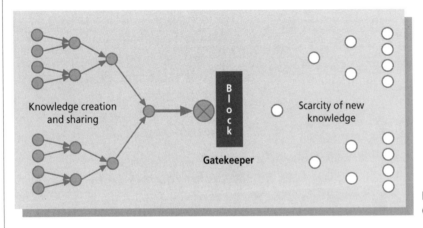

Figure 12.6
Gatekeeper role

This might be the chairperson of a financial approval committee, or the administration manager for a new ideas scheme. Wherever they sit, their criteria and rationale for taking decisions are likely to be based on past events, playing safe and taking a more traditional view of life. What happens then if the organization decides to invest time and money into a programme that facilitates the learning processes? In effect, the entire programme can be slowed down or stalled because a few people are able to block initiatives. This scenario gets worse the more senior the individual is within the organization. In the worst case, the board might consist of two or three people who are able to slow down the whole process of change and knowledge creation.

Finally, there are two problems that can face a blocker. The first is a sense of data overload – where the excessive amount of data input can lead to personal frustration and possible breakdown. The large volume of information and ideas flowing into the personal capital system may impact the agent's ability to select the most appropriate knowledge chunks that should be diffused.[4] Second, because they are tightly locked into the social and political system, change in structure can have a significant impact on their role – to the extent that the entire role might be at risk.

Creator / *Crank*

Acquire	Application	Age
Internal	Future	New

Figure 12.7

Upside – Creator

The development of a competitive advantage in the marketplace often hinges on creativity and invention – doing what others haven't yet done. Virgin's approach to air travel, Sony's mass marketing of the Walkman and Trevor Bayliss's invention of the clockwork radio are all examples of people using creativity and innovation to break the existing market mould. In most cases, this type of groundbreaking innovation enters market areas that others thought unworkable or unprofitable.

For example, imagine, sitting watching the TV, possibly something relaxing that can help you wind down and prepare for bed. All of a sudden a news programme comes on, one that raises the plight of people in Africa and the danger the Aids virus presents to them. The key issue highlighted by the show, is the need to build an effective communication infrastructure so that people can be educated about the dangers associated with the virus. Radio is the logical answer but the lack of electricity in remote areas makes this impossible, since the cost of batteries is so high. Of all the viewers in the UK, one person sits and ponders this dilemma and starts to ask questions about how this might be resolved. He starts to daydream about other devices that have been used to produce sound in desert situations. He imagines the old generals sitting in the sun during the Boer War, listening to music on their wind-up gramophones and wonders how this can be applied to the problem in Africa. All of a sudden he makes an intuitive link and realizes that clockwork radios might offer a solution.

From this idle daydream came the clockwork radio, an idea developed by the English inventor, Trevor Bayliss. The radio is now being sold around the world and is effectively helping to communicate the problems associated with the transmission of Aids in the poorer parts of Africa. It also provided a springboard for the development of a range of new products, such as clockwork lights, computers and a whole host of follow-on products by a number of large manufacturers.

The create profile might be applied to Trevor as he demonstrated the ability to cause something new to come into being, something unique that would not naturally have evolved without a creative input. This idea of creativity might be defined as something that evolves from one's own thought or imagination. Hence there is a synthesis of information between that drawn from the outside world and that which emerges from the deep tacit well within the individual.

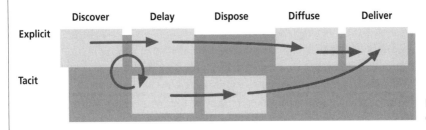

Figure 12.8
Creator profile

Although the creative role can never be defined as a fixed profile, an indicative model can be seen in Fig. 12.8. The assumptions are as follows.

- Often the creative process can be stimulated by explicit triggers from the outside world or the absorption of a small piece of information that becomes a nugget for future manipulation.
- The individual synthesizes this external trigger or nugget with current explicit and tacit knowledge help.
- There might be a degree of interaction between the short-term and long-term memory as the creator juggles with lost ideas and forgotten thoughts.
- Ultimately, once the delay process has helped to develop a new thought and knowledge, this actually goes back to the discovery stage as the creator has established a new form of knowledge.
- As part of the create process, the individual might have to let go or dispose of existing tacit ideas and beliefs so that new paradigms and mental models can be formed.
- Often, the creator will socialize and diffuse the idea with other people before taking it to market. This allows him or her to test its validity and enhance the knowledge through association with other close colleagues.
- Finally, the knowledge is presented to the world, ideally to create new and marketable opportunities for the inventor.

The creator role can be a difficult one to follow, especially within an organization. Consider the bland company statements that are posted on walls or included in the company values – 'we need innovation', 'everyone should contribute a new idea' or 'we have freedom to make mistakes'. These very explicit and overt statements are shadowed by tacit beliefs that change is hard; cover your arse wherever you can; and don't rock the boat. So the role of creator is one that can be seen to sometimes challenge and disrupt the status quo.

● Downside – Crank

Acquire	Application	Age
Internal	Future	New

Figure 12.9

The filter profile of internal focused, creating new knowledge for the future can also indicate someone who is passionate, focused and intense about the knowledge they are creating. Although this is a profile that would be valued by most companies, where it becomes extreme in nature it can result in a negative response. Where this negative response is seen, the creator is all of a sudden viewed as a radical or crank uttering nonsense who should be ignored.

Nowhere was this resistance to the creative role more apparent than in Galileo's promotion of Copernicanism in 1613. The creative challenge first surfaced when he wrote a letter about the problem of squaring the Copernican theory with certain biblical passages. Several Dominican fathers in Florence lodged complaints against Galileo in Rome and Galileo went to Rome to defend the Copernican cause and his good name. However, he was admonished not to hold, teach, or defend the Copernican theory 'in any way whatever, either orally or in writing'. Galileo was thus effectively muzzled on the Copernican issue. The end result was that Galileo was pronounced to be vehemently suspect of heresy and was condemned to life imprisonment and made to recant.

The warning for those who adopt a creator knowledge role is that they need to manage the profile carefully to ensure they are not seen as fools. Although the overt role is that of innovator, the secondary skills might be those of persuasion and political astuteness. Only by understanding the political system in which you are trying to create might it be possible to actually realize a market value from your work. The end result is that creators have to create value in two ways in the market. They have to both sell the content of their ideas and ensure that they are personally regarded as people with ideas that are practical and of value and not just crackpot ideas that should be consigned to the waste bin.

Director / *Dictator*

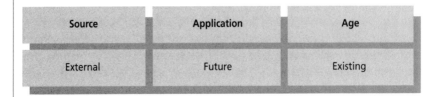

Source	Application	Age
External	Future	Existing

Figure 12.10

Upside – Director

In this profile, the role assumed is that of political or social leader or guide within a group. Now clearly, this can be a dangerous path to walk down since leadership is, by its very nature, a complex and confusing topic to consider. However, certain assumptions have been made about the director role. The first is that, in this role, the director is using knowledge as a process to lead or direct the group in a certain direction. Second, the whole team may commonly understand that the knowledge might be known only to the director. Third, that the director may or may not be formally directing the group. The director's position might be implicit in nature, or it might be an explicit and titled role. Finally, that the director role has to operate through a process of negotiated leadership rather than coercive and enforced domination. Consider the three examples of people who on different occasions used their knowledge as a tool to lead others.

Abraham Lincoln, the sixteenth president of the USA was almost entirely self-educated. In 1831 he settled in New Salem, Illinois and worked as a storekeeper, surveyor and postmaster while studying law. To win the Civil War Lincoln had to have popular support. The reunion of North and South required, first of all, a certain degree of unity in the North. But the North contained various groups with special interests of their own. Lincoln faced the task of attracting to his administration the support of as many divergent groups and individuals as possible. So he gave much of his time and attention to politics, which in one of its aspects is the art of attracting such support. Fortunately for the Union cause, he was a president with rare political skill. He had the knack of appealing to fellow politicians and talking to them in their own language. He had a talent for smoothing over personal differences and holding the loyalty of men antagonistic to one another.[5]

Mahatma Gandhi, was an Indian political and spiritual leader, called the Mahatma [great-souled] and regarded as the father of independent India. For Gandhi there was no dichotomy between religion and politics and his unique political power was in great measure attributable to the spiritual leadership he exerted over India's masses, who viewed him as a *sadhu* ('saint') and worshipped him as a *mahatma* ('great soul'). He chose *satya* ('truth') and *ahimsa* ('nonviolence' or love) as the polar stars of his political movement; the former was the ancient Vedic concept of the real, embodying the very essence of existence itself, while the latter, according to Hindu (as well as Jain) scripture, was the highest religion (*dharma*). With these two weapons, Gandhi assured his followers, unarmed India could bring the mightiest empire known to history to its knees. His mystic faith magnetized millions and the sacrificial suffering (*tapasya*) that he took upon himself by the purity of his chaste life and prolonged fasting armed him with great powers. The title *Mahatma* (great soul) reflected personal prestige so high that he could unify the diverse elements of the nationalist movement, the Indian National Congress, which he dominated from the early 1920s. After his death the methods of non-violent civil disobedience were adopted by protagonists of civil rights in the United States and by many protest movements throughout the world.

Martin Luther King was an African-American clergyman and civil rights leader. An active Baptist minister and a moving orator, he first gained national prominence by advocating passive resistance to segregation and leading a year-long boycott against the segregated bus lines in Montgomery, Alabama. Martin Luther King was a leader who was able to turn protests into a crusade and to translate local conflicts into moral issues of nationwide concern. Successful in awakening the black masses and galvanizing them into action, he won his greatest victories by appealing to the consciences of white Americans and thus bringing political leverage to bear on the federal government in Washington.

The three common elements with these leaders is the use of knowledge to direct others. For Abraham Lincoln, he used the knowledge of the political process as a way to unify disparate forces. Gandhi used his spiritual knowledge as a tool to create and sustain a leadership vision. Martin Luther King used knowledge of the racial problems and focused these at a deep level to raise consciousness. The common theme across these three approaches is the capacity to discover information at a deep and tacit level from the environment and to convert this into an explicit and open form of leadership.

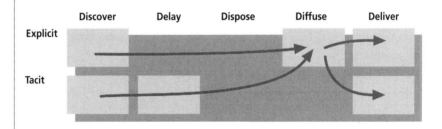

Figure 12.11
Director profile

The director profile as indicated might follow the following pattern.

● Explicit data is taken from the market that is pertinent to the problem being faced. This might be about the situation, or it might be environmental data that impacts the information.

● Tacit data is also acquired; often this will be an intuitive sense of what is happening and what is important to other people.

● This data is filtered through the current perception of what information is important and how it can be used to direct other people.

● This knowledge is diffused within a social grouping, to test its validity, gain social acceptance and take an opportunity to enhance its market value.

● Explicit knowledge is offered to the market as a form of guidance or soft instruction.

● This is reinforced by a tacit element that offers a more subtle form of direction to the market. This is often in the form of behaviour, with the person sending signals of do what I do rather than do what I say. It can also be in the form of tacit feelings, where the emotion signals the importance of the direction and outcome being advocated by the leader.

One of the common ways in which the director will lead and manage others is through the careful use of language. Directors play a major role in defining important issues and in influencing individual opinions regarding them. Political directors, in particular, can turn a hitherto relatively unknown problem into a major issue if they decide to call attention to it. One of the ways in which they rally opinion and smooth out the differences among those who are in basic agreement on a subject is by coining or popularizing symbols or slogans. Sir Winston Churchill popularized the phrase Cold War and the Allies in World War I were fighting 'a war to end all wars'. Slogans are among the most useful tools that are available to the political leader. Once enunciated, symbols and slogans are frequently kept alive and communicated to large audiences by the existing media and may become the cornerstone of public opinion on any given issue.

❝Symbols and slogans are frequently kept alive and communicated to large audiences by the existing media and may become the cornerstone of public opinion on any given issue❞

Downside – Dictator

One of the problems with this approach is that a director to one person will be seen as a dictator to another. Consider John Wayne and his long lasting friendship with John Ford. For many years John Ford coached and guided him through the Hollywood minefield, to the point where John Wayne had acted in over fifty B movies. At this point John Ford placed him in a lead role in a movie called *Stagecoach* which propelled Wayne to genuine stardom and won several Academy Awards. At this point the relationship changed and Ford was perceived as a tyrant and dictator who treated John Wayne harshly. Now, the assumption is that the director hasn't changed his approach, simply that others view him in a different light depending upon where they are sitting.

The same view might be offered about the three people highlighted as directors (Gandhi, King and Lincoln). Although many people will write about these people as individuals who led through example, passion and relationship, there are others who will view them as ruthless dictators, who managed others through stealth and political manoeuvring. The suggestion is that only you can decide what knowledge profile is appropriate for your situation. It might be that you aspire to use knowledge to lead others through the sensitive management of relationship, but they might view you as being manipulative and dictatorial. Again, the subjective way that knowledge is viewed suggests that you can never avoid this, but by understanding how fine a line exists between the two styles, greater attention can be paid to selecting on which side of the line you wish to stand.

Expert / *Egotist*

Acquire	Application	Age
Internal	Now	Existing

Figure 12.12

Upside – Expert

This is a knowledge profile that relies heavily on deep stored knowledge to create a market value. It is a person who has special skill or knowledge in some particular field. They posses a special kind of knowledge that is achieved through the devotion of time and passion to a niche subject area.

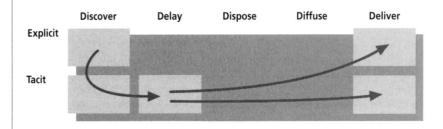

Figure 12.13
Expert profile

Although the knowledge content will drive the final profile model, there are a number of common key areas that might be found in a profile.

- The discovery of the knowledge will take place in both the tacit and the explicit areas. The need to take in at a tacit level is quite significant for this profile, since pure explicit knowledge would be less attractive than that backed up with a deep tacit understanding.

- There will be some knowledge stored in the explicit area, but the real market value will emerge from the tacit level. Anyone can read a book, yet it takes an expert to define the knowledge and make it contextually appropriate.

- The creation of a market value is notionally from the explicit stock, but ultimately long-lasting value will be driven by the tacit capability. Experts will draw a great deal of market value from the ability to act instinctively upon the tacit knowledge. Without any real thought they will make decisions, request action or take steps that they cannot even explain after the event.

Experts have a significant portion of their knowledge in tacit form (it is highly compiled). In many cases they do not reason from first principles, but trust their experience and gut feelings. They develop a sixth sense about what is 'good', 'balanced', 'quality', 'poor fit', 'out of place'. They use their tacit knowledge to detect subtle patterns and then associate interventions and repair strategies with these unarticulated categories. These patterns are quite special because, in many cases, they offer the real market value rather than the actual content of the knowledge.

One of the principal characteristics of experts in any domain is that they possess an extensive body of well-organized and highly differentiated knowledge. For example, an expert cardiologist can recognize very subtle differences between two medical problems that are very similar in presentation. This highly structured knowledge base enables the expert to use efficient and effective problem-solving strategies such as forward reasoning. This is characterized by drawing inferences from available data (e.g. as the doctor with a patient's symptoms) and moving forward towards the solution of the problem without having to explicitly test and evaluate hypotheses. This strategy results from having acquired and exercised knowledge repeatedly in particular contexts. This is in contrast to the novice physicians who will need to access more explicit referenced data to be sure of the decisions they are making. The one problem with this strategy is that it can be difficult for the expert to unpack the chain of inferences that are stored in the tacit memory. So the expert might make a rapid decision about a problem but not be able to explain how it was made and in many cases experts are not prepared to shift their views because the other view does not align with their tacit perception of the situation.[6]

Downside – Egotist

One of the problems with this profile can be seen in Fig. 12.13. There is little effort given to the disposal of old knowledge and as such the person can be seen as inflexible and stubborn when in this role. This inflexibility can mean the person is seen by others as someone who has too much investment in his or her own ego to let go of old ideas and move forward.

One interesting example of this type of spin might be seen with Albert Einstein, one of the greatest experts who ever lived. He once, famously, suggested that there is nothing accidental in nature. 'God does not play dice' was asserted again and again by Einstein in connection with his belief in a rational world of law and order and in his rejection of the appeal to random elements in certain forms of quantum theory, e.g. the so-called 'uncertainty principle' that is almost universally accepted. In insisting that 'God does not play dice', Einstein was accused of being a hard-line determinist. Although he was one of the leading figures in the development of quantum theory, Einstein regarded it as only a temporarily useful structure. He reserved his main efforts for his unified field theory, feeling that when it was completed the quantization of energy and charge would be found to be a consequence of it. Einstein wished his theories to have that simplicity and beauty which he thought fitting for an interpretation of the universe and which he did not find in quantum theory. Since then the undisputable successes of the quantum theory have convinced all but a handful of contemporary physicists that God does indeed play dice.

" 'God does not play dice' was asserted by Einstein in connection with his belief in a rational world of law and order "

I am not suggesting that either view is right or wrong. The point is that, although Einstein as a person possibly did not change, the world around him shifted, so that at one stage he is seen as a gifted expert and later as a single-minded professor who is not prepared to modify his views to fall in line with the accepted paradigm. Interestingly, it was such intransigence that helped him to develop his original paper on the theory of relativity.

The challenge with this profile is how to ensure that your market value is maintained, even when the market has shifted. The trick is twofold – first ensure that the discovery process is focused on the changing environment as well as the content of your expertise. Second, ensure that the disposal muscle is flexed, so that at times you are able to let go of the past expertise in order to create a new market offering that builds on the past and enhances your personal capital base.

Forager / *Freeloader*

Acquire	Application	Exist
External	Now	New

Figure 12.14

Upside – Forager

The film *The Great Escape* describes the real story of how prisoners tunnelled their way toward freedom with nothing but guts, perseverance and ingenuity. In the film, James Garner played the scavenger, the person who gathered the necessary information that enabled people to plan and execute the escape. In real life, F/L Des Plunkett and his team assumed responsibility for many of these activities. Real ID papers and passes were obtained by bribery or theft from the guards. A surprising number of guards proved cooperative in supplying railway timetables, maps and the bewildering number of official papers required for escapers. One tiny mistake in forgery, or one missing document would immediately have betrayed the holder, a problem complicated by the fact that the official stamps and appearance of the various papers were changed regularly.[7]

The forager is the person who forages outside the group and brings information, ideas and developments back to it. They will probably have masses
of outside contacts and are good at cultivating relationships. They are
rarely in their offices and when they are, they are probably on the tele-
phone trying to track down information or contacts. Although they are
the source of new ideas, the role is quite different to the creator because
they are conduits rather than sources of ideas. However, they do have the
ability to quickly filter out noise and they are quick to see the relevance
of new ideas.

Maybe one of the analogues for this type of role is the police investigator
whose objective is to examine, study or inquire into systematically the particulars of a situation. This is the type of role where an individual is asked
to search out and examine the particulars of a problem in an attempt to
learn the facts about something hidden, unique or complex. The contribution lies in measured and dispassionate analysis rather than creative
ideas and while they are unlikely to come up with an original proposal,
they are the most likely people to stop the team from committing itself
to a misguided project.

Although the role is slightly more convergent or critical in nature, they
do not usually criticize just for the sake of it, but only if they can see a
flaw in the plan or the argument. This, however, has the compensating
advantage that ego-involvement does not cloud or distort their judgement. Foragers are slow to make up their minds and like to be given time
to mull things over, but theirs might be the most objective mind in the
team.

One of their most valuable skills is in assimilating, interpreting and evalu-
ating large volumes of complex written material, analyzing problems and
assessing the judgements and contributions of others. Sometimes the passion for detail and correctness might appear to be less than tactful in style.
Also, the focus on investigation rather than solution might lead to a sense
of paralysis, but where the activity is controlled it can add real value to a
team.

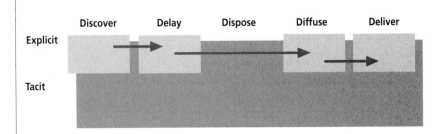

Figure 12.15
Forager profile

The primary profile assumption for this role is shown in Fig. 12.15 and can be summarized as follows.

● Information is discovered primarily through the explicit route, as they don't have long enough to develop an associative relationship.

● This incoming information is compared against knowledge held explicitly. This might be in the personal memory system or, in many cases, codified in some form of database or network.

● Diffusion takes place on the explicit level as they test and verify their conclusions against other people's ideas.

● Delivery is again at the explicit level, primarily because the role is a short-term activity, where the value is in producing fast, effective and actionable data for the market to use.

The scavenger role is one that is key to any group, but is often misunderstood. In many cases they act as the information tentacles that stretch into and beyond the organization, opening up doors and channels that other people might find impossible to unlock. However, there can be a problem when the scavengers lose a sense of personal balance. When this happens they can treat the providers of data as cold sources and not real people, as a result the suppliers always have the option to close down the gateways whenever they feel used or abused.

● Downside – Freeloader

One real danger is that the bravado and strength behind the forager role, when taken too far, can turn into the scrounger as played by the Artful Dodger in Dickens' *Oliver Twist*. Although the Artful Dodger is full of good intentions and beliefs, he becomes embroiled in a less than perfect situation. His role in the tale is someone who uses all the knowledge attributes of the forager, but they are focused on illegal activities.

In the story, he is seen to pilfer pocketbooks and handkerchiefs for his master and co-villain, Fagin. In this way he acts as a freeloader – someone who administers the flow of goods and ideas for an end receiver, but often without the appropriate knowledge to understand what is right or wrong according to the accepted norms. In my days as a field engineer, this role was seen in the person who was able to build a 'squirrel stock' of goods and items. They would spend a great deal of time building up a private and hidden stock of tools and products that could be used to bypass the formal stock management system. Although in the eyes of the local engineers this role was critical because it helped them to overcome problems whenever the stock system malfunctioned, the downside for the company was that the cost of stock holding increased and more time was spent managing redundant and damaged stock items.

❝ The line between forager and freeloader is a fine one and is difficult to define ❞

In simple terms, the freeloader can be seen as someone who tries to impose upon another's generosity or hospitality without sharing in the cost or responsibility involved. The risk with the forager role, is that we can get used to taking and fail to remember the point made earlier in the book about knowledge banks.

The line between forager and freeloader is a fine one and is difficult to define. Ultimately, it is down to you to manage the line, but much of the decision will be based on a simple acid test – always ask the question:

● Am I trying to obtain the knowledge by imposing on another's generosity or friendship?

● Am I gathering the information without intent to repay?

If either test proves true, then there might be a chance that the line has been stepped over and you are in the freeloader role. This is a valid role in certain situations, but the important thing is to know where you stand.

Possibly the reason why this role is so difficult to manage is because it operates on the explicit level as a data processing unit and does not have inner guidance from tacit experience. This facilitates a degree of speed and responsiveness, but can leave the owner without an inner rudder or guidance system. It is the tacit emotional value contained in the heart delay stage that gives the guidance, steerage and direction that help us make a conscious choice about that knowledge which adds value and that which constitutes an erosive element.

13

Managing the K-Profile

The great aim of education is not knowledge but action.

Herbert Spencer

O nce the K-Profile is in place, you will need to move from a build to a management phase. Ultimately, any management system must be defined, owned and tuned by you according to your goals and values. However, there are a number of common factors that might need to be considered to ensure that your knowledge is being managed as effectively as it might be.

Knowledge portfolio

The first point to build upon is something that has already been intimated in the book – namely that very few of us will have just one K-Profile. In most cases we will have different roles and this in turn means we need to identify what knowledge components are appropriate for each role. By classifying and mapping the knowledge groups we can develop and maintain a personal portfolio of knowledge assets. It might be that you choose to run a series of different maps, with each one tailored to specialisms where you want to create a market value.

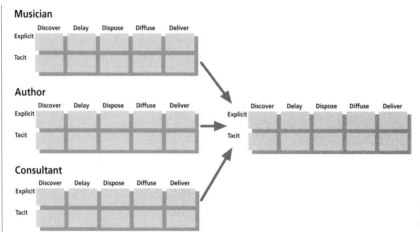

Figure 13.1
Personal portfolio

For me (at the time of writing), I tend to break my portfolio into three knowledge profiles: musician, author and consultant as seen in Fig. 13.1. (See the Appendix for examples of all three.) As a musician, my dominant delivery component tends to be explicit hand, as the primary market value is contained in my ability to play the guitar. As an author, the primary market value is in the explicit head component, as all you get in this book are my personal thoughts and mental models. Finally, as a consultant, the primary value tends to emerge from the explicit thoughts that are offered to the market, although closely followed by tacit heart, as much of the work I do is driven by personal passion to release the potential of others.

People generally run a portfolio life career for one of two reasons – because they were pushed or because they jumped. The pushed factor has been seen the world over as companies downsize, workforces restructure and the age of the part-time worker has come to the fore. In this case, we have little choice but to take on more than one job simply to pay the bills. The jumped factor is where people have made a life choice and to own their career decisions – so that they choose when to work and who for. Either way the outcome is similar, many individuals now focus on portfolio careers, moving from one project to another, where wide-ranging skills are required to stay competitive in the market. Ultimately, the goal should be the same – to maximize the value we can create in the market. The challenge is how the K-Profile can help to achieve this.

When in a portfolio career, your whole approach to life, learning and earning has to shift from the normal approach. The career ladder is generally no more. Linearity is out. A career is now a checkerboard, or even a maze. It's full of moves that go sideways, forward, slide on the diagonal, even go backward when that makes sense. (It often does.) 'Jobs' have become an obsolete remnant of the old world of work. The new world of work revolves around projects – an ongoing series of assignments that you take on inside one company, or an ever-changing portfolio of assignments that you complete for various clients. These projects teach you new skills, gain you new expertise, allow you to develop new capabilities, grow your colleague set and constantly reinvent you as a brand.[1]

Nowhere can this be seen to happen overnight more than in the entertainment world. In 1999, Geri Halliwell, formerly known as Ginger Spice, embarked on her new job as a United Nations goodwill ambassador to advocate women's rights around the world. Her volunteer work for the UN will not, however, get in the way of her career as a singer. Indeed, it may help her, since the UN may attract some press attention – and press attention is valuable to an entertainer. She used the knowledge capability to manage relationships to leverage and build a new K-Profile as internal ambassador.

It is a function of our media-rich age that we are expected to turn fame, even notoriety, into cash. Celebrities cash in by building brand equity – name recognition – and then attaching that equity to some saleable product or service. It could be a book, a speech, a doll or a line of latex house paint. Today's big stars no longer rely on just one revenue stream. The hot entertainers are platinum-level singers who become bestselling poets and movie stars. Or athletes with record companies and fashion lines. Or rap moguls who establish sports agencies and toy companies. All have their sights on building brand equity, much the same way Coca-Cola or Buick builds brand equity.[2]

So, the question might be how can the K-Profile help you manage your personal portfolio. I suggest that portfolio management is about three core things.

- First, manage the portfolio interaction to highlight synergies, where two or more components can reinforce the total brand value.

- Second, manage the portfolio to ensure that one knowledge component does not act as a liability for another profile.

- Third, use the profile as a tool to identify where new career options might be built into the portfolio.

The first idea is to use the portfolio map to create internal relationships that multiply and create new value. In my research for this book, I interviewed many people to understand what portfolio mixes people managed. It always amazes me how much untapped potential existed in the people's personal capital base. I would meet engineers who were deemed to be lacking in personal motivation, only to find that they ran football clubs at the weekend; or the engineer who transferred across into the sales team, but never created the chance to use his unique front-line perspective in selling the company goods and products. What the sales team and the company failed to do was to recognize how the skills and attributes from the engineer's parallel life could be used to enhance current operations. A personal example of this compound interaction came from the realization that my musician and consultant profiles can and do interact. Before using the profile tool I used to believe that the two roles were quite separate and in fact caused significant problems because of the conflicting time demands. However, I now actually use my music as part of the learning process when running courses. The integrative process helped me understand how I might differentiate myself in what is a highly competitive market. The reality is that there are many millions of consultants in the world, many of whom fight for the same clients. However, there are fewer who are able to use music as a teaching tool. This approach really helps me to create a differentiator in the market and one that allows me to increase the pleasure of the time I spend in each profile.

The second idea is to understand how conflicting elements in the portfolio can degrade the overall market value. Consider the portfolio worker that is running three primary roles: marketing consultant, business school lecturer and non-executive board member of a small start-up company. In theory they should all be non-conflicting roles, but he starts to have problems when inconsistency occurs between his role as consultant and board member. One of his selling points as a consultant and lecturer is the sense of independence that allows him to offer more open and radical views on certain areas of business. He plays very much on his tacit head angle – drawing upon his many years of experience to give open advice to clients and delegates. However, this strong tacit view causes problems as a board member, where the other members of the board are looking for someone who is willing to play a more open and explicit game and not take intuitive decisions. This causes a conflict, where he struggles to swap roles as he assumes responsibility for each position. Does he try to develop both approaches and run them in all the roles, or should he take the view that it is better to develop and enhance one of the approaches?

Finally, by mapping and managing the different profiles within your portfolio, you can start to understand what gaps might exist in the total package. So, to pull upon my personal profile of musician, author and consultant, where gaps exist at component level I have a range of choices. The first is to simply accept the gaps as natural; to focus on enhancing the components in isolation, maybe to improve my ability to dispose of tacit heart knowledge; or develop a new profile that draws on the missing components. For example this might be a simple case of developing a role in which I can occasionally help out with charities or local businesses to enhance my ability to disengage from close emotional relationships.

If the recent economic changes have triggered this shift to a portfolio approach to careers, then it behoves each of use to re-think how we manage our careers and personal development within such a framework. No longer can we measure our personal value and worth in life by the latest job title or parking space slot. We must start to use systems that will help define our value as seen across a range of diverse and differing income streams.

● Knowledge strategies

In the same way that organizations might define knowledge goals and strategies to create their own future, so we as individuals must develop knowledge strategies. We must be able to plan, map and understand what knowledge we will need in the future so that we maintain control of the discovery process and do not fall into the habit of discovery through chance and happenstance. We need to develop a clear strategic intent that will set out where we want to go and what steps are necessary to achieve the appropriate market value.

Strategic choices

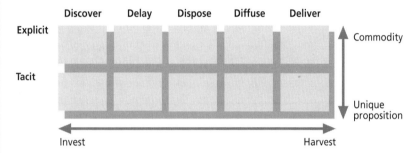

Figure 13.2
Strategic profile

Personal capital strategy is ultimately about choice and consequences. We all make decisions about the future, the problem is that often we aren't aware of the decision being made and, even worse, don't understand the implications of the resolution. The strange thing is that we are less inclined to take the same approach when talking about our time, finance or health. It is unlikely that we would spend two days of our personal time on a project that yielded no payback; I know of few people who would be prepared to invest their personal savings into something that gave no practical or aesthetic return; and although many people do take poor decisions regarding their health, it is generally on the basis that they understand the consequences (of the next cigarette or bottle of wine). So why is it that we are happy to invest our time, money and personal energy in the acquisition and delivery of personal capital that is at best of limited value and at worst a liability.

One of the first things to understand is where we should apply the most effort within the K-Profile to realize our personal and professional goals. Now clearly the final action plan will have to funnel down to a deep level – to understand what specific knowledge acquisition and delivery actions have to be delivered over a certain time-scale. However, the first stage is to consider the four key-areas within the profile and decide where the most time and energy should be allocated.

Explicit investment

In focusing on this strategy, your goal will be to accumulate, market and store ideas, techniques and information that exist in the market in codified form. This might be by acquiring a professional or industry qualification, attending a specialist course, or simply reading a series of books by a preferred author. The upside with this strategy is that the options are generally wide ranging, the market is often over supplied so costs are low and most options can be tailored to fit your personal situation. The downside is that, if you can access the information, so can anyone else. The challenge is that, in focusing on this segment, you must still have the output in mind and be aware of how you can use the codified information to create something that is uniquely yours.

Tacit investment

In taking this route, your goal will be to acquire and store deep knowledge that you can in turn make unique for you. Once you have absorbed and internalized this knowledge, no matter how you apply it in the open market, it will have your scent and flavour. The investment process for this segment can be time consuming, expensive and painful. By virtue of the fact that you absorb the information through experience and intuitive judgement, this is not something that can be gleaned from a book. The reward is that you will be able to create a strong USP in the market. The risk is that you might pick the wrong knowledge area, or even worse the marketplace might have moved on by the time you are ready to sell your wares.

Explicit harvest

With this intent, your goal is to recoup the market value of the investment made in your personal capital base. In drawing on the explicit knowledge base you will be using clear and codified knowledge that can be readily replicated and used by others. If your strategy is to focus on this area, you might be writing a book, publishing articles, presenting conferences, designing new processes, or running training courses. The end result will be that whatever you put in the market will be available to others to copy and replicate as they choose.

Tacit harvest

If your aim is to focus on the tacit level, then your intention will be to create value in the market that is differentiated and cannot easily be replicated by others. As a strategy, this can harvest high reward and long-term gain, one of the difficulties can be in communicating your value proposition. If the market is to reward you for your deep and non-replicable value, then how can you describe the value you are going to offer? Consider two project managers who are about to apply for a position to role out a large IT programme in a European bank. Applicant A markets her value on the explicit proposition, explaining the change strategies and project tools that she will use to manage the programme. Applicant B markets his value on the basis of experience and hands-on management of a range of programmes. Whereas A can explain her strategies in a matter of minutes, it might take B quite a long time to explain the deep strategies that he uses to manage change programmes. So, the tacit harvest strategy can be effective, but you will need to think through how to position it in the market so that people can understand the value, even if they don't understand the content of the delivered value.

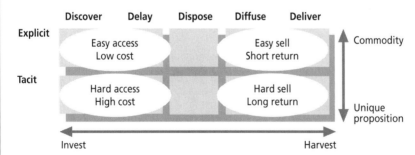

Figure 13.3
Strategic options

The whole point of this exercise is twofold; first understand where you sit at present; and second, define where you need to sit in order to realize your goals. My guess is that if you were to reflect on how you allocate your time and money at present, you would probably have a bias towards one of the four quadrants. It might not be a heavy bias, but there will probably be an emphasis on one of the four domains. If this is so, one of the first steps within your strategic planning process will be to understand where you should sit and what action you might take to move into that quadrant (Fig. 13.3).

Strategy gravity

Having a strategy is one thing, but as anyone who has tried to diet or give up smoking will testify, it's sustaining the intent that proves to be difficult. However, the greatest cause of 'intent corruption' can often be ourselves. Though, in many cases, we develop clear structures and strategies to achieve the required knowledge, deviations and distractions take us away from the intended direction. This deviation can feel like a remote gravity or black hole that exerts a pull over us.

Consider the young graduate who has a clear goal to achieve a first degree and then use it to become a city trader. At this point there is a straight line that connects the individual intent to the end knowledge goal as seen in Fig. 13.4.

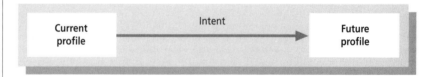

Figure 13.4
Strategic intent

All goes well until he becomes interested in the new and emerging subject of chaos theory and its impact upon the stock market. Over time, he spends more discovery resources on this area. He reads all the latest articles, talks with physicists at college and attends lectures on the emerging sciences. Now, this knowledge does have value, but it is a value that is contextually appropriate. The people who will be recruiting for the areas where he wants to work might respect his personal capability to look at future market systems but, unfortunately, they are looking for basic competency to trade and manage a desk. Although his intent is still in place, much of his valuable time has been misdirected into low value areas.

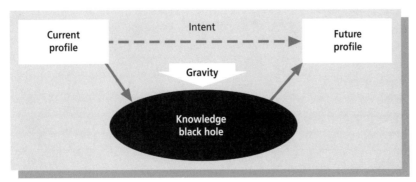

Figure 13.5

This can be seen in terms of a black hole that has gravitational pull over the knowledge strategy. If you make a personal choice about what knowledge will be appropriate in the future, then it is important that extraneous forces are not allowed to drag you away from this end goal. This is not to suggest that creativity and serendipity should not be allowed to flourish, but ideally this should be directed towards the end goal and not just a random permutation that might not add any real value.

Strategic options

This book will help you map and build a set of personal K-Strategies. As such, you should consider the following.

Personal orientation

This is the classic 'know where you want to go before setting off on the journey' question. In the knowledge sense, it is the need to be clear on what type of knowledge you want to acquire and this must fit in with your business and personal goals. Although much of the focus of this book is on how knowledge can create market value, we must still understand how this fits within our personal values and goals.

Asset base

At some point, the knowledge profile must be completed to truly understand what assets you currently own. Although you might intuitively guess at what personal capital you have, often it is only the processes of deep analytical reflection that will really bring out the current knowledge assets and liabilities. Unless these are captured and used as a base line, then any planning process will not be grounded in reality.

Environment

Since one of the main problems of strategic management is coping with uncertainty, it is useful to begin an analysis of the environment by asking (a) How uncertain is the environment? (b) What are the reasons for that uncertainty? (c) How should the uncertainty be dealt with? Only by understanding these three issues can you start to build a personal capital system that minimizes the chance that changes in the environment will erode the value of your knowledge growth.

Scenarios

Ensure that any strategy draws upon the idea of potential scenarios. Don't simply select a future knowledge position and assume that it will be appropriate. How on earth can you hope to develop a plan for the future when no one can predict what the future will be? One way to deal with this is to develop scenarios or potential stories about how the future might turn out and what your role would be in that future. By articulating what might happen tomorrow, you can develop the ability to make more appropriate and practical choices today.[3]

Costs

Be clear as to the resource requirements and costs that any knowledge strategy will drive. Although the availability of free information is increasing with the growth and stretch of the Internet, the reality is that any knowledge acquisition will incur a cost in some form. This might be the loss of personal time; the charge to attend a conference; or the basic cost of a PC to access the Internet. Unless these cost and resource implications are understood and linked back to the discovery process, then it is probable that we will suddenly find holes in the knowledge profiles, as we are unable to find the time or money to acquire a new knowledge chunk.

Performance measurement

Clearly, unless we have a process to measure the performance of the knowledge we acquire, there is little chance of managing the changing processes within the strategy. If you plan to spend three years acquiring business expertise from an MBA programme, you must constantly reflect on the knowledge acquisition content and process to ensure that it really is delivering end value and personal benefit.

Strategic alliance

Try to plan and understand how you will need to link your knowledge to others to deliver the end goal. Although you might view yourself as a knowledge island, very few of us create true market value entirely on our own. We generally all draw, in some way, on the knowledge and expertise of others to deliver our personal value to the world.

K-Profile strategies are difficult things to define, manage and deliver – simply because they are so personal. It might be that you have the personal discipline and strength to set out a strategy and keep to it, but in many cases human frailties will step in to make this difficult. If this is the case, then try to develop support structures that will help you to maintain the knowledge strategy. This might be by asking your partner to help; through the use of a personal coach; or the use of a diary or digital assistant to track progress. Only you can define what system will work for you, the important thing is to have one that will work and to have a clear outcome in mind.

Strategy delivery

The goal is to develop an outcome or strategy you feel will really grow value in the future. The danger lies in developing a strategy with an end goal that is vague and blurred, almost a 'just make things better' statement. You must be able to draw out a realistic, tangible and measurable strategy and be sure that you have both the desire and the capability to deliver the end goal. You can help achieve this by asking seven simple questions in the OUTCOME framework.

Owns – who owns the outcome and is it self maintained?

Ultimately, the question is do you have the desire and capability to manage the knowledge change or will other external forces be able to erode any movement forward? Do you hold all the levers (financial, time, resources, etc.) or are you dependent on others to help make the shift forward.

Unease – what triggered the need for change?

Ask why you need this new knowledge and what priority does it hold over other issues?

Trade-off – what will you have to give up to achieve it?

One often-forgotten fact is that we adopt certain policies or behaviours because there is a payback. Delivering a new knowledge strategy means that something will have to change and something will have to be lost. You must think through and appreciate the potential loss before you can commit to any new personal strategy.

Changed – how will life be different when the change is made?

At this point you should test the value of the new knowledge by clarifying what new value will be created once the knowledge has been gathered. Take a mental step forward in time to consider how life will be different at the end of the project, to imagine what language will be used, what the environment will look like, what the productivity figures will be – anything that helps you to actually 'be' in the future.

Others – what impact will it have on others (losers, winners and neutral)?

In effecting a new personal strategy, one of the dangers is that short-term and urgent forces are being responded to and little attention is paid to the impact that any change will have on other people. It is important to consider 'all' people that are affected by any change and to possibly consider them in terms of winners, losers or neutral. From this you should be able to offer a realistic picture of who will be affected by the proposed change and, more importantly, what reaction can be anticipated.

Measure – how will the new knowledge be measured?

How will you know if the acquisition has been successful? To be sure that the strategy is one that you really want and can achieve, you should be able to describe in simple terms how you will 'know' that it has been delivered.

Engage – what is the first step?

The hardest part in any personal strategy is the first step or the point of engagement. The danger is that personal change is always put off until tomorrow. So at this point it helps to say what your first action will be to engage the knowledge strategy and to make it real.

Once the strategic outcomes have been clearly defined, you need to focus on the detail of the strategy – to understand what specific actions you will need to take within each of the five stages (discover, delay, discard, diffuse and deliver). Most importantly, ensure that you have the necessary resolve and stamina to manage the transition through to its completion and not to be waylaid by diversionary forces.

Personal capital coaching

Coaching might be defined as a process by which an individual helps another person realize his or her desired potential. This might be in a work situation, where a line manager has been asked to help one of the team make the first step into a management position. It might be in a home situation where your partner or child wants to take up a new hobby or life skill. Alternatively, you might be a football coach working to help one of the team improve his or her playing skills.

However, there are three problems that can cause the coaching process to flounder and in many cases fail to really help the coachee make the personal change. First, it can be difficult to quantify the specific changes that the individual needs to make. Second, it becomes very easy for the coach to assume responsibility for the change process and so take implicit responsibility of the transformation. Lastly, both parties can slip into an idealized dream state, where the outcomes aren't really grounded in reality.

The primary goal of any coaching process is to help coachees think through what they want to achieve and how they might achieve it

The primary goal of any coaching process is to help coachees think through what they want to achieve and how they might achieve it. However, once it gets into the detail of action planning, it can become difficult to define explicitly what steps need to be taken. This can be because the coachee hasn't really thought through the detail of the change, or the coach doesn't have sufficient understanding of the content and context of the change situation being considered.

Any coaching situation can end up being managed by the coach. Although the coachee will sometimes take responsibility for managing the process, in many cases they will resist any form of challenge or confrontation and hence push the responsibility back onto the coach. Where this occurs it also means that the coach takes responsibility for the learning process, which consequently limits the chances that the individual will maintain the change on a long-term basis. If any change is to be sustainable, then the coachee must be helped to own the learning process and in particular take real responsibility for his or her knowledge currency, stocks and flows.

Finally, if the coaching process is to be grounded in a sense of reality, then the discussion itself should take place at the level of knowledge action rather than at the level of visionary goals and objectives. Most people will quite happily sit down and describe what their goals are for the next three years, but ask them to describe what specific knowledge will be required to achieve that goal and the process can become somewhat harder. Every New Year's Eve, millions of people will happily tell their friends that they are about to lose weight, give up smoking or stop drinking. Ask them what exactly they will stop eating, or what they will do when the urge to have a drink or cigarette kicks in and there is less chance that they will have a firm response.

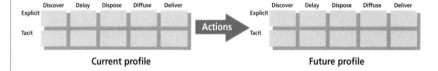

Figure 13.6

Current profile → Actions → Future profile

The key message underpinning these three points is that, for change to be real, the coachee must own the learning and knowledge management process to a manageable degree. Use of the knowledge profile will give both the coach and coachee a valuable tool by which they can clarify understanding, map the future position and agree what specific actions can be taken. This process is given added power if the discussion can take place at the level of specific knowledge actions that the individual will take.

Although the knowledge coaching process will vary according to the process and individuals involved, there are three core stages that can underpin any effective knowledge coaching process.

Knowledge inventory

The first step in any change process is to understand where you are at present. Unless you have a clear understanding of the asset base and market value at the outset, then it can be difficult to agree how and where the end goal should be. The key points to consider are as follows.

Map the assets

One of the problems at this stage can be the temptation to get sucked into mapping the more tangible areas. It can be relatively easy to codify the explicit head and explicit behaviour areas for the five stages in the model. It is a lot harder to help the client to map the other areas, especially if they are not used to the profiling system. One of the ways to do this might be to complete the first profile for the client. Rather than asking clients to describe what assets they have in the different areas, just get them to talk about what they do; how they do it; and how others would describe their asset. While they do this you can slowly start to map the profile from your perspective. Once the first cut version is formed, then you can hand it over for them to complete in more detail.

Balance sheet

It can also be tempting to focus on the more positive aspects of the profile. Helping someone to understand how their knowledge actually acts against their self-interest can be difficult. Someone might have spent many lonely nights and weekends to get a speciality degree and your challenge that it has only limited value might not be well received. However, unless we understand our knowledge liabilities as well as our assets, the final change process will at best be flawed and at worst will collapse completely as we fail to make any headway towards our goal.

Step into the shadow

Finally, in determining the current state, it is important to unearth some of the shadow knowledge. This is the knowledge that owners prefer to hide from the world or themselves. These are the undiscussable issues, such as failed exams, negative feelings towards another individual, or skills that they sell but don't really have. Surfacing these can be difficult for the coach but, unless they are surfaced, barriers and obstacles can arise later once they start to emerge.

Knowledge goals

At this point you can start to help the coachee develop a view of what goals he or she wishes to achieve and from this define what knowledge bases or personal capital will be necessary to fulfil that goal. If the person's wish is to become a concert pianist, then by the end of this stage he or she should have a clear profile that sets out what currency and stocks are necessary to achieve this outcome.

Play games and tell stories

We often develop a future state and then get locked into the view that this is the only viable option. When trying to build a future goal that is practical and owned, it is important to broaden the options as widely as possible and to consider all of the potential outcomes that might be achieved. To do this, help coachees to talk about what they might achieve through the use of metaphors and stories. Try to help them visualize what potential things they might achieve on the basis that no constraints existed to prevent them from moving forward. Once a range of options and stories have been explored, you can then help them to funnel down and select the most appropriate outcome.

Delivery components

Once their outcome is clear, you can start to build the second profile. This one will translate their outcome into a tangible K-Profile that is representative of the end state. If the individual wishes to become a concert pianist in five years, then you need to consider the delivery stage of the map and what knowledge components will have to be in place and where possible take this down to the detail of specific knowledge chunks.

Profile components

Once the components that make up the market value have been set, it becomes possible to complete the rest of the profile. This will involve identifying what knowledge will have to be discovered; how it will be sorted; what old ways of working and thinking need to be discarded and who they need to socialize with to grow the knowledge. By this stage the coachee should have a complete 'to be' profile developed.

Knowledge actions

At this stage, the profile will be completed down to chunk level. For each component in the profile, it is now possible to undertake a gap analysis. For example, the 'as is' explicit head diffuse component can be compared with the 'to be' component. The end result will be a series of knowledge chunks that need to be acquired and disposed of. For each knowledge chunk, coachees will have a clear understanding of what needs to be achieved; its viability and how it can be accomplished.

Define K-chunks

In undertaking the component gap analysis, the final stage is to define clear and unambiguous K-chunks that need to be addressed. So, yet again for the aspiring concert pianist, in the diffuse tacit heart component, there will possibly be a need for two separate actions. First, build close relationships with other pianists who will be able to offer honest feedback on his or her skills; and develop close associations with agents who will promote the concert and develop the capability.

Check opposing forces

As the old maxim goes, for every action there will be a counter action. If the action is to be effective you need to ensure that the coachee defines what opposing forces will be generated against the knowledge actions. For example, if the K-Chunk action is to build relationships with the concert agents, question what will prevent this from happening, why would they not want to build a relationship; and then define what steps can be taken to overcome these barriers.

Confirm action, desire and capability

The final step in the coaching process is to help the coachee firmly commit to the planned changes. So often the knowledge management process is taken lightly and as a result intent is not transformed into market value. We attend a course, go to conferences, or read books and then assume that knowledge has been acquired and can be used to good effect. As the five-stage model shows, the acquisition or discovery stage is just the first step in the journey to creating market value. If coachees are serious about developing their knowledge profile, then coaches must test out their desire and capacity to take the knowledge through to the delivery stage.

Coaching is a powerful tool that can help people manage their life transitions, yet it is also a process that can cause frustration and confusion when promises aren't kept and action plans fail to materialize. If the coach does not help the coachee to understand what end knowledge and capital will be required to achieve the end state, then little is likely to happen. If you are coaching a colleague, friend or partner, unless you take the time to measure the future knowledge against the future goals, then your and his or her time might end up being seen as a future gesture. This doesn't need to be a laborious process, even asking a few questions about how the person will need to think, feel or behave in the future can help that person to understand how difficult the change can be and what specific actions he or she needs to put in place.

Team profiles

As I dare to offer yet another way that teams can work more effectively together, I can almost hear you run screaming from the room with tears in your eyes. However, I hope to offer a way of looking at teams in a slightly different way. Not that the existing tools don't have value, but I suggest that, for teams to work effectively, they need to understand how to manage their knowledge effectively as well as their behaviours.

The knowledge profile can be used with a team in the same way that it is with an individual, the only difference is in the build. This can take place in at least three ways: construction of the team members' individual profiles and then simple amalgamation through an additive process; or, construction of the collective team profile through a shared experience; or a synthesis of the two, where individuals complete their profiles separately and then debate how representative the summation is of the team's personal capital and market value.

In my view, the process you use is driven by the need for the profile in the first place. If the objective in developing the profile is to obtain a summary map of the team's personal capital, then simple amalgamation will offer a basic idea of the amalgamated market value. However, by taking a simple additive approach, many of the softer factors can be lost. If your team is actually a collection of individuals who manage their own suppliers and customers, then completion on an individual basis will be representative of the team's natural style. However, very few teams actually operate in this way. They exist as a team because the combination of a select group of people is seen to add value to them and the organization. It is this magic ingredient that will be lost if people complete the profile separately.

The second option is for the team to meet and debate how they believe the team in totality can be represented in each of the knowledge components. This will generally be done through a process of open debate and dialogue, where the goal is to surface all of the knowledge capital, as described by the team and the customer base. However, while this does help the team to develop a shared appreciation of its collective capital, there can be major problems in trying to surface some of the deeper issues that need to be included. The reference to shadow knowledge earlier in the book is a good example of the knowledge that can be omitted from the final profile. Just imagine you are sitting in a room with a team of colleagues where the objective is to agree the real value of the knowledge of the people in the team. Although some mature teams will be able to complete this exercise, in the majority of cases the team social, political and historic issues will surface shadow action, or lead to the inclusion of knowledge on the profile that is incorrect.

The final option is the synthesis between the two ways. This is a two-stage process where team members complete the profile on their own. This can be a loose process where people are given some guidance and left to complete it in their own style, or you might choose to engineer a process that utilize all of the typical team development processes, such as 360-degree review, and facilitator support. Once all of the profile is complete, the next stage might be to share the profile with the team (named or anonymous) for pre-review and then meet to consider the data. The upside of this approach is that the final profile is likely to be richer and more honest about the real value of the team's personal capital. The downside is that it can take longer and if the full support processes are used, can be more costly.

At the end of the process, as a minimum, you would have each person's knowledge profile and a shared schematic model that indicates the team's total personal capital. Now it is possible to take this in many further directions, all of which are dependent upon the team goals and resources constraints. The first option might be to share the profile with customers or suppliers to get their view and from this feedback modify the content of the profile. Another idea is to build a 'to be' map for the team, indicating what knowledge needs to be in place within a specified time frame. Alternatively, you might wish to undertake some best practice analysis by comparing the profile with that of a similar team inside the company or in a comparable unit in another business. Finally, you might choose to undertake a risk analysis, to understand what the implications are for the team if certain members leave. Hopefully you should get the idea that the team profile can be used in as many ways as you might use any other team instrument. The difference in this case is that the core purpose is to understand what shared knowledge the team holds and, more importantly, how this creates value within the organization.

Depending upon the maturity and goals of the team, the K-Profile can be a powerful tool to use in mapping and resolving internal team conflict. Although people try to address intra-team conflict by looking at personalities, tasks or management styles, it might be that the disagreement is being driven by inconsistent knowledge management styles.

Profile	Source	Application	Age
Apprentice / *Amateur*	Internal	Future	Existing
Broker / *Blocker*	External	Now	Existing
Creator / *Crank*	Internal	Future	New
Director / *Dictator*	External	Future	Existing
Expert / *Egotist*	Internal	Now	Existing
Forager / *Freeloader*	External	Now	New

Figure 13.7
K-Profiles

If we consider the six different roles that were introduced in the profile stage as shown in Fig. 13.7, it is possible to identify where certain dynamics in the way people manage knowledge could clash.

Consider the idea of the apprentice working for someone with a creator profile. Although the first two filters match, there might be a problem with the type of knowledge being used. While the apprentice is simply trying to play catch-up, to understand what he or she needs to know in order to perform effectively today, the creator is thinking way downstream. The creator is trying to generate new ideas and knowledge that will be applied in two or three years. Now the apprentice profile should not be seen as just a formal process of internships leading to accreditation. It can be seen in the two-week orientation period that a new person will go through upon joining a company. Now, consider the typical R&D or marketing team who are focused two, three and in some case ten years into the future. These groups are, by their very nature, future-focused and the creator profile will be the dominant one. This can lead to a problem when new people join the group as they are trying to understand the 'as is' situation and ground themselves in the current situation, while their colleges are off in the distance. When this situation does occur, it can help to surface the idea of the K-Profile which can help us understand that we sometimes need to put one profile away and run with a different one so as to help colleagues join the team.

" The K-Profile can be a powerful tool to use in mapping and resolving internal team conflict"

Another possible clash can be seen when the creator works with the expert. Whereas the creator is future-focused and trying to originate new ideas and knowledge, the expert is working from a current stance, in the belief that the knowledge they have at present will create the most market value. This situation can be compounded if both parties move into their shadows, where they work together as crank and egotist. If this happens, the walls go up and meaningful conversation becomes almost impossible. In this case the first step is to help them to understand the K-Profile they are using to undertake their job and then to highlight what causes the clash. Once understood, there is a greater chance that each will tolerate the other person's assumed profile and they can attempt to operate in a more collaborative fashion.

As you might imagine, the list can go on – both using the profile table shown above and using any profiles or filters that you might have thought of. However, the goal is not to create stereotypical conflict situations that you can look out for. The objective is to demonstrate how our preferred knowledge management process could trigger off conflict in teams. If you find that your team is showing signs of conflict, then try using the K-Profile as a tool to draw out where the areas of conflict are coming from. Where possible, encourage others who are experiencing problems to draw their joint profile and flesh out what areas operate in sympathy and what areas are conflicting.

Mergers and acquisitions

Bigger is better is the oft-heard refrain of companies announcing merger plans. In pursuit of economies of scale, the merging companies race to integrate their assets and prove the wisdom of the union to the financial institutions. But while many companies hasten to integrate tangible, fixed assets, they often overlook the critical task of integrating their intellectual assets. As a result, they forfeit much of the value of merging.

Before companies make any legal agreement to join up, they compare balance sheets, evaluate marketing strategies and identify operational redundancies. Very few take the time to define and understand how their corporate units learn. Even fewer try to determine how the bringing together of different learning styles will impact upon the company's ability to generate and manage its personal capital. All too often companies neglect to evaluate the knowledge cultures – a synergistic element at least as important as the financials – until well after the ink is dry on the binding agreement. Let's get the numbers and marketing pitch in sync, the prevailing sentiment goes, and worry about the people part later.

Consider the tale of two large global companies. Company A plays the role of valiant acquirer, rescuing Company B from a hostile buyout by another company. Intent on making the merger pay off, A's executives concentrate on reducing costs. They eliminate fixed assets and reduce the headcount. The theory is that one marketing team can sell both companies' products? But in consolidating the marketing teams, they fail to consider the relative value of each individual and base layoff decisions entirely the good guy and bad guy syndrome. People are dispensed with purely on anecdotal views of how effective their last project was. When the merger is finalized the company simply hands redundancy notices and severance pay to all the people who are not required.

Within weeks of the layoffs, the folly of this decision can start to surface. In firing people on an arbitrary basis, the company has dismissed people that had the most valuable personal capital. As the story suggests, it is terribly easy for senior managers orchestrating a merger to get stuck in an Industrial Age mentality that focuses on reducing operating costs by shutting factories and wholesale layoffs. But companies that want to develop long-term, sustainable competitive advantage had better safeguard their intellectual assets. As the knowledge economy evolves, Wall Street is responding by valuing companies on their ability to deliver innovative and creative products and services. Although many merging companies, dive right into managing fixed assets, it's more critical at the outset of a merger to concentrate on retaining, synthesizing and maximizing intellectual assets.

Merging companies that create a system to maximize the value of intellectual assets and corporate expertise are much more likely to flourish. When culture clash hinders the integration of the knowledge and experience of both organizations, mergers are much more likely to fall far short of the expectations originally predicted by senior management. Here are concrete steps senior managers can take to avoid culture clash and help ensure the effective integration of intellectual assets in merging organizations.

Many companies just don't understand that the employees who are considered the most valuable for their productivity, innovation and knowledge are often the first to look for other employment once a merger is announced. CVs are dusted off, job sites on the web are accessed and head-hunters scour the fertile landscape and are quick to pounce on a company's best employees if they perceive that morale is lagging or the future is uncertain. Often the most creative and innovative employees are the ones who attempt to survey what the merged organization will look like and, if they are not confident of their place in the new organization, they will seek other opportunities that will keep their careers on track.

Even after managers have successfully cultivated a climate of trust, knowledge sharing may not occur if employees don't know who has the expertise that could help them do their jobs better. To facilitate information sharing, companies must first identify employees from both organizations who have expertise in areas that could benefit the combined business. By compiling that information into a database of internal experts, the expertise of both organizations can be made accessible company wide.

As the knowledge economy continues to develop, the importance of capitalizing on personal capital will only increase. Fixed assets were built to become extinct; every time they're used, a small part of their value vanishes. Intellectual assets last as long as they're handed down; every time they're used, the experience becomes more valuable. Few business challenges demonstrate the importance of this lesson more clearly than mergers and acquisitions. Although intellectual assets are particularly vulnerable during such times of transition, no company can afford to ignore the task of safeguarding the irreplaceable knowledge and experience of its employees.[4]

However, although knowledge is the most important asset of any company, managers are often stumped on how to deal with something that cannot be quantified, let alone universally defined. My suggestion is that by using the K-Profile system, companies can start to define and manage some of the knowledge that can be controlled during a merger or acquisition.

The tool can be used in the following ways.

Expert mapping

When planning or executing a merger or acquisition, start to identify who the perceived experts are in the key business areas from both sides of the venture. Use the K-Profile to map their personal capital. Use the final profiles to draw conclusions about their roles in the venture and what can be done to ease any problems and where possible create synergies. Consider, where their expertise comes from; how it is stored; if it can be codified and shared with others or if it's stored at a deep tacit level; and finally, what the cost of replacement is should the individual leave during the merger.

Role integration

Following a similar process to the previous idea, where you know that certain roles will have to be integrated, it makes sense to map the K-Profile of the existing incumbents. If the point of the merger or acquisition is to build on the knowledge synergies between the two companies, then this philosophy and action must take place at the lowest level within the company. By mapping their K-Profiles for the roles you can draw upon the ideas of the existing players to build a new profile, one that adds real synergistic value to the integration and does not end up being a political bun fight over whose existing procedures and processes are best.

Team integration

In many cases the merger or acquisition process will lead to the integration of teams – often from different national homes. However, so often the integration process tends to operate at process level – often in the guise of 'my process is better than yours and if you don't agree I will tell my boss' (who is the new VP). It can help to understand the knowledge factors that will impact upon the team integration. Consider how they currently discover new knowledge; where it is stored; do they operate at tacit or explicit level? These are all issues that will surface once people start to work together, therefore it will help if these items are considered during the merger process. If this can happen, it can help to follow the process outlined earlier, where each team builds its own profile and these are then shared at a joint K-Profile meeting involving the key players from each base team. From this, the new team leader can start to build a 'to be' profile that defines how the team should manage knowledge in the future.

Exit interviews

By their very nature, most merger or acquisition processes will result in the loss of people who no longer fit in the new company. Often these people are paid off and simply leave – walking out of the door with their stock of personal capital. It might be more practical to use the K-Profile to map people's personal capital before they leave so that at least some form of intellectual legacy is held within the new company.

In supporting the merger or acquisition, the primary objective is to ease the process by which the companies come together and, more importantly, to exploit the accumulated personal capital of the new group. No one tool can do this in isolation, but use of the K-Profile will raise our consciousness about the need to effectively manage knowledge.

How can leaders make priorities for alignment without first understanding the diverse knowledge of the merging organizations? Culture clashes, differing intellectual approaches, learning preferences and product and service expertise need to be understood as part of the merger or acquisition. The K-Profile enables more accurate valuation of the knowledge element, which will improve the likelihood of merger or acquisition success. Determining the likely scale of integration, duplication and potential areas of difficulty as part of the due diligence process will cost a fraction of the whole preparation and will tackle issues which research show are at the heart of successful or unsuccessful integration.

By simply undertaking a sample of organizational know-how using a tool like the K-Profile, it may be possible to predict the outcomes of merger or acquisition activities. Poor planning produces poor results and, in the K-Profile, the merger or acquisition environment now has a tool to help with the integration process.

14

Measuring personal capital

The hours of folly are measured by the clock,
but of wisdom no clock can measure.

William Blake

The surest way to determine your value is to sell it. The income you are offered reflects whether your value is greater than your judged market value and adds value to the cost of knowledge discovery. That happens during mergers, acquisitions, buyouts and whenever company stock is traded. The value of a company's knowledge can be explained as the difference between its reported financial assets and its actual market value, which is the share price multiplied by the number of shares. In the same way, the only real way in which you can ultimately understand your true value is by placing it on the open market.

The 'value' of the personal capital defines the market worth that an individual can create in the open market. The critical issue here is the notion of the open market. So often we can slip into a time and space warp – where we value our personal capital against the local environment, rather than understanding how much importance is placed upon our knowledge in the open market. If you value yourself as a commodity, then you will trade as one if, however, you value yourself in terms of a unique brand proposition, then true market value might be realized.

Nowhere has this rampant disconnect been seen more than in the software industry during late 1999. The growth of e-commerce triggered a serious shortage of skilled workers who could offer a combination of strategy, marketing and technical ability. The scarcity of these skills led to a situation where e-experts could almost name their own price and this price spiralled exponentially at an alarming rate. One company who were looking for this type of expertise noted that 'we hold our breath when we go into negotiations now, wondering what people are going to ask'.

So many times I have seen the situation where a company employee has worked for a large corporation for fifteen years and has this particular blend of skills. However, because such employees measure the value of their personal capital on the internal rate of pay, they are blissfully unaware of their market value. Only by understanding a true measurement process do they start to understand the value of their personal capital and so negotiate the appropriate reward inside the company.

In essence, they are developing their personal value in terms of the book valuation, i.e. what value the company ascribes according to the capital investment, rather than what the asset is worth on the open market. To manage the difference and to realize a true and fair return for your personal capital, the only option is to continuously measure the value of your capital by whatever means is appropriate for you, rather than what the company ascribes.

This part of the book considers why you need to measure your value; some of the structural elements that might be considered; and what factors might cause a problem. This is with the caveat that there is no one simple and all encompassing way in which to measure your capital value.

Why measure personal value?

Intriguingly, by developing a measurement process you will grow your ability to understand and manage your tacit capability. So often, the tacit element of the K-Profile is hidden and embedded because we don't have cause to measure its market worth. By making the process a conscious one we start to make this core part of the system visible. I know that the discipline of playing at gigs and getting paid for them gives me valuable feedback on my market worth as a musician. I might sit in the bedroom developing new and commercial songs but, at the end of the day, it is the willingness of the public to pay to hear the songs that helps me to understand how much the tacit is really worth. At the end of the gig, by talking to people I get a real feel for those parts of the songs that were valued and those that were less effective. This type of intuitive feedback helps me to understand how the market is valuing my tacit capability.

Another benefit is that measuring the value of my output or knowledge delivery helps me to understand what new knowledge I should acquire to enhance the capital base. So software programmers who measure their worth in terms of the languages they are able to write can track and map the market trends, so that they know when to shift the focus onto new software tools and languages.

Building on this understanding, the measurement process will aid the prioritization process, or identify where time needs to be spent on discovering or delaying the knowledge base. So often I have seen people acquire new skills or personal competencies that are clearly focused on what they want to do rather than what they need to do. One example is people who go to college to gain a particular qualification, even though it is poorly regarded by the market and will lose market attraction over time. My guess is that we take this type of decision because we are input rather than output focused. We think about what we would like to do know, rather than ask the question what can I learn that will give me market value.

Once you understand the true rather than imposed value of your personal capital, a gradual realization will occur that you own the knowledge footprint. So often we ascribe that knowledge that we have to the company where we work. We assume that because we work for a widget company, the company owns that knowledge about the construction of widgets. In the knowledge era this is a defunct and obsolete model – now you are the ultimate owner of the knowledge of the production process and unless you are contractually restricted from sharing that knowledge, if you walk so will the personal capital. As you start to realize the true value and worth of the knowledge, so a greater sense of ownership will be fostered. As you start to own and manage your personal capital, so the company will benefit as you take time and energy to nurture and enhance this personal knowledge base. This produces a synergistic relationship between the employee and employer. In the same way that, historically, people would take pride in a job well done, they might now take pride in personal capital that is well managed.

One of the major growths in recent years seems to have been in the conference market. Barely a week goes by when I don't receive an armful of brochures proclaiming how the next conference will add value to me personally and help my company take the next leap forward into future markets. As an occasional presenter at these conferences, I find it highly amusing to challenge people to justify the money they or their company has spent on the event. The truth is that few people equate a monetary investment in this type of event with a corresponding change in their personal capital. The whole idea is again front-ended, where people look at the input stage without thinking about what corresponding shift will take place in the personal capital. This is a simple example of the malaise that exists across industries worldwide where people don't measure value and hence never truly understand the benefits accrued from a training or development programme. If we are to manage personal knowledge, then the process of measurement will in itself make the change and improvement explicit. One of the ways in which this knowledge change can be measured is by using an added value approach – where the change in stock is measured rather than the value of the output.

Map elements

At the heart of the measurement process is the capability to match the elements in the delivery stage of the K-Profile to the market. In essence to understand what knowledge chunks reside in each unit of the model and what value the market would ascribe to that unit.

The aim is to place a market value on both the explicit and tacit elements of the deliver stage in the K-Profile. Now clearly, there is a risk here of over-egging the pudding and even getting to a state of paralysis through analysis – where more time is spent deconstructing your knowledge base than growing or enhancing it. Ultimately, we must always understand the reason for measurement is to manage the asset, not to create a measurement process.

The first step with this process is to define what is to be valued within the K-Profile. Taking each area, we consider the delivery stage of the map and consider what knowledge sits inside the explicit and tacit elements. In the case of marketing managers, in the explicit head component, they will have a range of specific knowledge chunks. By taking each of these chunks we can start to understand what the open market is paying and what type of supply and demand factors are operating. The source of this information will be wholly dependent upon the market in which you operate. It might be that fast and accurate market prices are available through surveys and publications in trade journals. If you operate in more niche areas, then the data might be gathered through conversation with peers and colleagues. Alternatively, you might simply approach a job agency armed with your core competencies and ask it to define the market value. No one answer will be correct, but the outcome will be of more value than a commodity value that is arrived at by comparing your pay with that of colleagues in your company.

As we take each of the components in turn, it becomes possible to undertake a zero-based knowledge build, basically re-constructing the individual around knowledge chunks – where each chunk is understood in isolation and in relation to the other components. In this build process, we develop the capability to both match competencies against the market and experiment with ideas of how the total market value might be enhanced. So, if the explicit area were to include knowledge of another language, what would be the best language to learn and what value would this generate?

This leads to a critical part of the map – that of negative deployment. Whereas so far the whole focus has been on measuring the added value elements of our personal capital, we must be honest and realize that certain elements of how we think, feel and behave can actually destroy much of the value we have embedded in a personal capital system.

So, it might be that we have knowledge about markets; how to run a marketing team and have read all the books on managing relationships, but this might fall apart when we walk into a meeting room. If the tacit components don't support the explicit value, then the value can be eroded very quickly. Conversely, we might have a deep-rooted ability to run a marketing team but, unless we are able to describe how we do this (hence have a gap in the explicit part of the map), we might be unable to convince the senior team to offer us new opportunities and projects. The end result is that we all have a personal capital balance sheet, one that indicates those knowledge assets that add value and those which destroy personal value or brand.

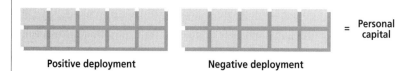

Figure 14.1
Knowledge balance sheet

When you get to this level of deconstruction it can become very personal and difficult. Since knowledge is essentially a contextual thing, what is a positive to one person will be a negative to another. So, for mechanics, knowledge about a particular car will be highly advantageous in one country, but if they travel to a country where the car is not popular then their knowledge might be devalued overnight. At an even deeper level, cross component issues can mean that a knowledge chunk is a positive and a negative at the same time. So, imagine Jim who has a deep capability to develop close relationships (tacit heart). When he uses this capability in his role as a sales manager, it adds immense value to his overall personal proposition, however, he also spends evenings as a counsellor at the local drug centre. This ability to get close to people means that he becomes overly involved with the drug addicts and as such cannot carry on in the counselling role.

This example leads to another factor that plays a significant role in the K-Profile – the need to understand the portfolio balance. The nature of the roles we all have in life can have a significant impact upon the value we create in the market. I know of one person who had an amazing capability to build relationships with people both rapidly and at a deep level. Over a period of time I started to build his K-Profile, but when looking at his work profile in isolation, we couldn't understand where this capability came from. Only when we broadened the scope to consider other life profiles did we understand the source of the knowledge. It turned out that he spent much of his personal time as a supporter with the local church and as a result developed the capability to develop close relationships grounded in deep and honest principles. So in measuring the output stage, we also need to understand the input factors that can drift across from other knowledge profiles.

Added value measurement

Although output measurement offers a view of the value you might be able to generate in an open market, it is also important to understand how effective you are at managing and creating knowledge. So, on the assumption that knowledge flows through you like water through a plumbing system, do you know how efficient and effective your knowledge management processes are? Are you able to take incoming information and effectively convert it into products for the market with minimal overhead costs? Can you take information and add innovative value so that a totally new product is created as a result of your internal processes? Are you aware of the knowledge losses that occur as you try to process different knowledge streams and products? and To what extent can you use background and maintenance activities as levers to enhance your knowledge stock?

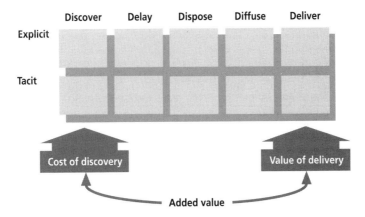

Figure 14.2
Knowledge added value

Figure 14.2 indicates the basic added value model. On one side of the K-Profile we can see the input or discovery stage. On the other is the market delivery. In between the two something will happen to the flow of knowledge. This might be that it is incorrectly held in the working memory and as such is lost to the ether. It might be that it is deliberately discarded on the false assumption that it has little value. Alternatively, you might have inadvertently socialized it through the diffusion process and, as a consequence, eroded its market value. Any one of these three stages can cause the value or content of the knowledge to be eroded or lost.

Alternatively, if you have an effective management system in place, you might be able to use the same stages to realize an accumulation of the value or content of the knowledge. In the delay stage you might develop the capability to rapidly transfer knowledge from short- to long-term memory and access it on demand. For the discard stage you might develop the capability to stay adaptable and flexible in a changing world and discard redundant mental models that restrict your ability respond to change. Finally, you might develop a powerful network of colleagues so that your diffusion process allows you to grow and enhance ideas before they are offered to the market.

Ultimately, the effective management of your added value between the discovery and delivery stages is as important as your capability to discover or deliver knowledge in the open market. You might have all the right acquisition and deployment skills, but if your personal management processes are inefficient, then your personal capital will be eroded over time. Although the steps you can take to manage and measure this added stage are many, some of the more significant ones are listed below.

● Know how you know

As any proficient process engineer will tell you – the first stage of any process improvement is to run an 'as is' analysis. Map how you process knowledge and what the key stages are within the process.

Know how you decide

The decision-making processes you apply drive the way you manage knowledge flow to each stage. How do you decide what information to store and what storage processes are best for different types of knowledge? How do you decide when to push the 'delete' button on your e-mail system and so destroy all that possible archive material? How do you decide who to share your latest big idea with? and How do you know if they can be trusted not to share it with anyone else?

Know the interfaces

Although much of the knowledge you process through the five stages will be managed internally, there will be certain types of knowledge and situations where you interface with other people. This might be the expert who can give you advice on a certain topic, or possibly your partner when you talk through your woes at the end of the day. It might be that these people have a significant impact on the speed and quality of the way you process knowledge and any impact needs to be understood. For example, does you partner take a more cautious view of life than you and therefore influence you to be more risk adverse than you might naturally be.

Know the support systems

At some stage in the processing cycle you will probably be dependent upon someone or something else outside the process to manage the knowledge. This might be an outsourcing process where your personal assistant takes responsibility for storing or retrieving information. It might be a dependency on a certain type of IT system or web tool to retrieve data. Whatever the system, unless you understand how it impacts upon the flow and what risks it brings, your capability to manage the knowledge might be restricted.

Know the critical variables

Since the K-Profile is built upon the premise that we are all different and our knowledge maps and processes will be unique, we need to understand how certain process factors might impact the management process. When under time pressure, do you become more prone to forgetting things or pushing the delete button? When high quality is required, does this impact on your ability to process with speed? or When you need to apply more effort to a certain project does this mean that other priorities suffer?

Know the key cost base

Some of us are able to process knowledge rapidly and effectively with only cost incursions, while others tend to have a higher cost/output ratio. This cost might be driven by time, where your personal style might be analytical and unhurried and as such you take longer to process knowledge than other people might. Your cost base might be higher because you have a greater reliance upon external processes and machinery. The fact that your cost base is higher does not mean that you are automatically disadvantaged, it does mean, however, that you need to understand the implications if you are working in a team or competitive situation.

Know the critical measures

Finally, the point of discussing all these issues is to understand what stage points need to be measured. Ask yourself: How much time do I spend on discovering new knowledge? How good is my working memory at retaining new ideas? How often do I delete files from my e-mail system? and How much time do I spend sharing knowledge with other people and what value does it realize?

The whole reason for measuring these seven areas is not to install a superlative control system. The idea is that you should have explicit and intuitive knowledge of the effectiveness of your processing capability

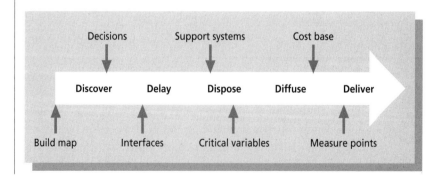

Figure 14.3

and the measurement data is simply one of the tools by which you can make changes to your knowledge management style. Unless you are always prepared and motivated to re-engineer how you manage your knowledge flow, there is a chance that you will be overtaken by others who have developed faster or more effective ways to process their knowledge.

One clear way that the capability to add value across the five stages is becoming ever more important is in the field of e-business, through the seamless transfer of data and information over open and closed networks. It is this rapid movement of information, combined with the ability to bring separate groups together both inside and outside the organization, that makes e-business so powerful. Perhaps the biggest selling feature of e-business is the ease with which it can be deployed throughout an entire supply chain. It effortlessly links manufacturers, assemblers, distributors, marketers and customers. As the rate of change speeds up, companies will need a dynamic blend of skills and experience to succeed in e-business. Success will depend on embracing new technologies, understanding current business processes and having a clear vision of how future ones will work. If you sit in the middle of this supply chain, your personal capital process will have a significant impact on the efficiency of the e-business processes. Often just one person can act as a significant amplifier or gate within the whole process. It is all very well speeding up the flow of information through the company channels, but if it all slows down when it reaches a particular individual there will be little chance to recoup any value from the investment.

Key elements

When using the K-Profile, there are a number of underlying factors that need to be considered.

Currency exchange rate

The value you ascribe to your personal capital might not be the same as the value the market offers. While you may think that you have a set of ideas and skills that are of significant value, if there is little fit with the environment they will realize little market value. One of the areas where I have seen this occur on a regular basis is the contextual difference between academic and operational learning. So often I have seen colleagues spend years and years studying for their degrees or MBAs, only to have them rubbished when they get back to the workplace. The context in which they acquire new knowledge is seriously undervalued by the workplace – and in many cases can deter the individual from doing any more studying. Hence to realize real market value from the learning experience, they need to consider a number of potential options. First, help the organization value the knowledge by marketing the operational aspects of the college course; second to take the knowledge elsewhere, by changing jobs. The final option might be to convert the academic knowledge into operational knowledge by a conversion process (for example running an internal project).

Timing

Clearly, knowledge is something that can have immense value one day and then lose it overnight as the market changes. Just think about how many people you know who are living on the legacy of historic knowledge, but fail to realize the limited time they have before it becomes redundant. The implication this has on the measurement process is the need to increase the rate of measurement. In a static market, we might be able to measure on a yearly basis and retain sufficient currency. However, for someone who operates in a dynamic world such as the advertising or software industry, the measurement process might need to take place on a monthly or half yearly basis. Take this to the extreme and consider the ticket touts standing outside the local rock venue – their knowledge base changes dynamically on a daily basis. As such they have to be totally in tune with the current value of their knowledge and develop systems and procedures that measure it accordingly.

Capital interaction

One thing that can impact on the measurement process is the interrelationship between the various knowledge components. As already considered, it might be that you are delivering value to the market that is dependent upon two or more components within the map. The problem is that the measurement process might be driven by one component and this does not truly reflect the value offered by the other components. Think about the last time you saw a charismatic presenter at a conference or on TV. His or her offering was probably based around a number of critical success factors. First might be the explicit head factor of the knowledge offered to the market; the explicit behavioural skills used to present ideas; and the explicit and tacit heart capability to offer ideas with enough passion to change the world. Now such presenters could place a market value on the ideas they offer to the world by the number of articles published and books sold – but how does that indicate the value of the passion used to present the ideas? The danger is that the presenters might measure their personal value on the explicit head component and not really understand or measure the other factors. So, when the books stop selling, they might assume that the problem is a failure in the models offered to the world, when in reality it might be that the audience had become bored with their rambunctious style of presentation. So the explicit behaviour erodes the value offered by the explicit head models. Unless their measurement systems are able to track the various ways in which the components create value in the market, then there is a danger of over and misjudged compensation in the way they attempt to regain market presence.

Method

Another aspect to consider is the style of measurement. Should the process be a quantitative model, where hard quantitative data is returned, or is a qualitative framework used which offers softer and more subjective measures. The quantitative measure can be very numbers driven and indicate how many courses you have taken or the scores achieved. However, this is a really dangerous measure and one that is abused. The use of quantitative measures can lead to people trying to achieve the measures rather than trying to change the culture. It can also create a false sense of end goals, i.e. 'I have met 75% of the criteria so I can back off now.' The qualitative approach is concerned with the change in personal capital from a subjective position. This type of measure might be drawn from interviews with people after they have been through an experience with you of personal reflection on the deep changes you have fostered. In real terms the optimum position is to try to go for a mix of the two. The quantitative elements will help sell your market value to others, whereas the qualitative elements will help you to reflect on the changes you have made and plan to make.

You might also need to consider how to measure the value embedded in your relationships with others. There are times when something inexplicable happens between two people – a manifestation that would not have happened to an individual. Every time you sit down to discuss options and ideas with a client, you have the chance to create new relational capital. It is the existence of this social asset that offers so much hidden value. All organizations have particular capabilities for creating a market advantage and this is often found in the space between the people. Your role is to grab the capital that exists in your relationship with others and use this to create a market advantage.

" Every time you sit down to discuss options and ideas with a client, you have the chance to create new relational capital"

The relational delivery process can take place in two forms, either at the tacit or explicit level. Tacit relational knowledge exists where people that work together over a period of time improve their working methods but may not recognize or discuss the improvement. Examples are musicians who play together for a long period or comedians who intuitively grow their appreciation of each other's style and preferred methods of working. Alternatively, relational knowledge can exist at the explicit level. Examples are researchers writing a paper together or a project team where people share ideas in building the project plans. The problem with measuring this type of value is the integration of your value with other people. Consider just how many successful partnerships break up only to find that without each other their value is destroyed overnight.

To measure your value within this type of situation, you might try to draw three maps as seen in Fig. 14.4. Draw your K-Profile, your partners profile and then build a third K-Profile which is a representation of the synergy between you. This will not give a definitive value to people within the relationship (as if such a thing is possible) but will start to help with the analysis process and help break value down to a knowledge chunk level.

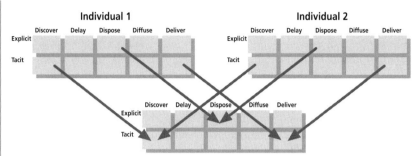

Figure 14.4
Relational value

Ultimately, the whole measurement process is a real minefield and one fraught with real danger. The risk is that you can start to build and develop systems that produce at best erroneous and at worst significantly incorrect measures. You must always understand that measurements exist to gauge progress, not to drive the change process. The push should come from your desire to understand your personal value, not to build a master measurement system.

Potential problems

As with any measurement system, the saying is generally easier than the doing. The problem with such a process is that it incurs resistance. Similar problems can surface when you try to use a measurement process on your personal knowledge system.

I suggest that we all have some degree of natural reticence to measurement as it surfaces the lows as well as the highs. No one likes to think that they have a gold-plated level of knowledge in a certain field; only to discover that their expertise is quite limited against the market or will become out of date in a few years. Often we can drift along in an organization, appearing to be blissfully happy, only to find that all of a sudden an unexpected crisis will surface that we struggle to resolve. This is because we often hide parts of ourselves from the organization, from our colleagues and from ourselves. This phenomenon is known as 'defensive routines' and has been extensively covered by Chris Argyris since the 1970s. They might be defined as routines used by both the people and the organization to keep themselves deliberately in the dark so as to avoid unpleasant surprises, threats, or anything that might be construed as uncomfortable.[1]

This idea is neatly encapsulated by the Johari window,[2] a model that offers four simple views of people's personality and behaviour. The proposition is that people can be considered through four different windows: (1) the self we share with others; (2) the self others see but which may not be known to the individual; (3) the private self that others don't see; and (4) the self hidden from both the individual and others. This can be represented as seen in Fig. 14.5.

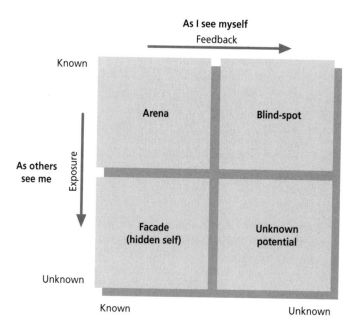

Figure 14.5
Johari window

This diagram offers a simple overview of the model and helps to identify the four quadrants that need to be carefully thought about when considering the balance between the open and hidden self.

Arena

The arena is the person that both the individual knows and all of his or her colleagues will recognize. Examples might be the hobbies people have, the number of children, the type of food they prefer or their feelings on a particular topic. This is the quadrant where ideas can flow, learning occurs naturally and the organization holds on to the ability to grow its capacity to initiate surprises.

Blind-spot

This is what other people know about the individual, but the individual is not aware of it. This might be the irritating habits that people have, or the way they look. Whatever, the attitudes or behaviours that sit in this quadrant have the potential to cause conflict with others and to block the process of knowledge and knowledge creation in an organization. Consider a colleague trying to share an idea who has such irritating habits that there is a tendency to avoid spending time with him or her. This will cause a breakdown in the sharing of knowledge and a subsequent loss for the business.

Facade

This might be seen as the hidden self. It is those areas of the personal life and personality that the individual does not want to share with others. This might be the fact that they have recently been divorced or are having problems dealing with a dilemma at work. Again, this area does not help to generate a spirit of creativity and learning. If individuals are unable to share themselves with others, there is less chance that learning or surprises will emerge in the interaction with others.

Unknown potential

This is the undiscovered self, the area that no one knows about. It is this area that Carl Jung talks about as the unconscious area that might not be seen, but acts in such a way as to influence the behaviour of the individual. This can be seen in a positive and negative light. It might be that the unconscious 'other in us' can suddenly emerge in times of stress. For example, shouting at the children after coming home from a hard day's work, or walking out on the job when things get rough. Alternatively, it might be where a person has the latent and innate ability to play an instrument but time and fate have prevented him or her from ever taking the opportunity to find this out.

One point to note about the Johari window is that the four quadrants are not static. They will vary depending upon who the individual is with at the time. Consider the first time an individual meets a new director – the arena is likely to be more closed down than when he or she meets a known manager.

This process of changing the size of the quadrant is driven primarily by two actions. As individuals start to expose themselves, so the arena and hidden self boxes will enlarge. As a result, there is more chance that others will give feedback on their perceptions of the person and hence the arena and blind-spot will again enlarge. In doing this, there will be an automatic reduction in the size of the unknown potential box. However, on getting this feedback, there is every chance that individuals will invoke a series of defensive routines so as to protect themselves from being damaged by other people's unfavourable comments.

So, if you are about to build your K-Profile, a number of thoughts might be considered. First, however hard you measure yourself; assume that you are still not focusing on the area that offers the real problem in managing the flow. Second, try to get feedback from colleagues or friends on how well they believe you manage the knowledge process. No matter how introspective you try to be, there is always a chance that something will block the flow – and this is something that can only be seen by an observer. Finally, don't assume that the measure will be static. Although it might measure the process, the nature of the knowledge flow is dynamic – and sometimes rapid. So the knowledge you have of yourself today will be different to that you had yesterday and will have tomorrow, hence any measurement system must be dynamic enough to stretch and flow the window as it changes shape.

Finally, I offer a closing view that might seem to be in contradiction with much of the content of this chapter, but only serves to offer a counterbalance to the risk that you might start to over-engineer your K-Profile.

In many ways the whole suggestion that knowledge should be measured might be seen as a foolish idea. If we consider that the area of high value is often in the tacit stock – this is the part that is unique, embedded, difficult to externalize and is intrinsically wrapped up in our beliefs, values and schematic view of the world. The very process of trying to externalize this knowledge might in itself devalue or corrupt any external value that can be applied. Think of the last time you went to a library or searched the Internet. The choices you took to decide which book or paper to select are intrinsically wrapped up in your deep tacit models and structures. I believe that, given sufficient time and energy, I could map and measure your decision-making process – but to what purpose?

" The very process of trying to externalize this knowledge might in itself devalue or corrupt any external value that can be applied"

Measurement must be done with reason and outcome in mind, not with a goal to build a measurement system. It must be a core element within any K-Profile system, but a factor that is subordinate to the process, not the determinant.

15

Epilogue

This knowledge I pursue is the finest pleasure I have ever known.
I could no sooner give it up than I could the very air that I breathe.
Paolo Uccello

The accepted wisdom is that knowledge management is a critical necessity because what worked yesterday may or may not work tomorrow. Companies that were manufacturing the best quality buggy whips became obsolete regardless of the efficiency of their processes since their product definition didn't keep up with the changing needs of the market. However, we must now move beyond the notion of knowledge management at a corporate level and take it down to the level of the individual. Unless you too take urgent steps to manage *your* knowledge, then, like the buggy whip manufacturers, you might be consigned to the sidelines while peers and junior colleagues achieve their goals and you can only look on and gaze with envy and regret.

My belief is that the K-Profile will help you to avoid falling into this trap. It is a practical tool that will help you enhance your capability to learn, manage and market your personal capital. From this, I hope you will be able to enhance your personal brand value. However, if you find that the K-Profile as a tool does not add value, then I hope that you accept the spirit and intention behind the model and take the time to build your own personal knowledge system. Although you clearly must build and fashion a system that is fit for your purpose, I would suggest that many of the thoughts covered in the book and listed below should be included somewhere in your thoughts:

❚❚ The K-Profile is a practical tool that will help you enhance your capability to learn, manage and market your personal capital ❚❚

- What filters do I use that enhance or block my ability to acquire knowledge?
- How do I create new knowledge?
- What investment strategies do I employ that ensure I acquire value added knowledge?
- How effective is my memory as a storage system?
- How do I use systems to retain information?
- What impact do emotions have on my storage capability?
- How do I store knowledge in partnership with other people?
- Have I developed my capability to unlearn?
- How do I manage the pain that goes with letting go?
- What strategies do I have to ensure that I can modify knowledge on my terms rather than being forced by someone else?
- What explicit and intuitive processes do I use to share and transfer knowledge with colleagues?
- To what extent do competitive forces impact on my ability or desire to share knowledge?
- To what extent do I buy and sell knowledge as a tradable entity?
- How do I use communities of interest to amplify and enhance my personal capital?
- Can I place a market value on my personal capital?
- How do I balance the relationships with my employer and the market?
- Where do I position my personal capital in the market?

Finally, now you have reached the end, I offer you a genuine challenge: What will you do with the information contained in the book? Can you put the content to good use? Is it worth storing for retrieval later? Can any of the ideas be used to leverage your personal value in the market-place? This challenge is a real one because, unless you ask these questions and take the appropriate decisions, you have potentially wasted a valuable chunk of your knowledge acquisition time and in the knowledge era this is something that few can afford to waste.

Personal K-Profiles

Consultant	Discover	Delay	Dispose	Diffuse	Deliver
Explicit					
	Research programmes	Filofax log	Reading diverse books from non-related areas	Team meetings	Change models
	Web Listservs	Books	Challenge from peers	Writing articles	NLP tools
	Product design with team	Home filing system	Meals with Paul Oliver	Personal network of contacts	Articles and books
	Client feedback	Long-term memory	Failed bids	*Need to grow learning network*	MBA
	Books	Laptop for paper and ideas		E-mail updates to colleagues	Professional qualifications
	Professional articles	Psion for short-term retain		Web site	New management tools
	Conferences	Client management system			Outcome tools
	Writing	*Need to improve hard system for filing long-term papers*			Seven Cs framework
	Need to take broader cultural perspective	*Need to increase client reviews to get feedback on ideas*			Lead yourself before leading others
	NLP masters course	Refresh from running courses	Feedback from clients and courses	Share training style on courses	Presentation skills
	Sales course	Refresh as delegate	Team learning sessions	Share facilitation style in work days	Facilitation skills
	Peer feedback on coaching	Personal diary	Guidance from practice head		Negotiation skills
	Need to listen more and leave space for others				
	New tools from Sara Rowe				
	Client feedback	*Need to catalogue client records and track emotional status*	Letting go of fixed beliefs in design sessions	Close team network to share emotions and feelings	Personal three year goals
	Discussion with life partner			Close client network to share feelings	Client network
	Discussion with team				Many years experience of a range of business functions and markets
	Need to learn how to socialize better with new clients				Associate network

Consultant	Discover	Delay	Dispose	Diffuse	Deliver
Tacit					
	Client association Life experiences Bid development Dialogues with Paul Oliver		*Need to step outside comfortable market sectors* *Need to lose some preconceptions about the technology limitations in knowledge transfer*	Dave Chitty helps to ground and test my ideas	Understanding of industry Personal principles
	Coaching from peers			Working with team members	Capability to build trust
	Personal reflection Socialization sessions *Need to lose subordinate feeling to ex-bosses*		Had to move from a position of job in large company to free agent *Need to lose dependency on children*	Team beer bust and dinners help to build relationships Relationship with mentor	Willing to give open feedback Sensitive to others' emotions Outcome focus

Musician	Discover	Delay	Dispose	Diffuse	Deliver
Explicit					
	Listen to radio for new songs Talk with friends about new gigs Jamming with Gary to create new lyrics and songs New gigs from taxi driver	Log song list on database Printed version of song list to take to gigs Lyrics stored on word files Database access to lyrics and music Midi files available on web	Need to move outside favourite song domain and look for other types of songs to play	Web chat lines E-mail with gigs and other musicians Talking at pubs and other gigs	Quality of original songs Quality of selection with cover songs CD sales CD with 'Lead Yourself 'book
	Listen for new styles of playing Watch other bands and acquire skills		Need to shift from analogue to digital style of recording	Playing in jamming sessions	Musical skills Range of styles
	Tune in to those songs that people whistle Find bands where there is a buzz	Remember the old songs that people still like Keep relationship with old agent and gig managers	Have to let go of desire to play favourite songs all the time	Finding great songs and sharing with band	Relationship with gig managers

Musician	Discover	Delay	Dispose	Diffuse	Deliver
Tacit					
	Feedback from gigs on what songs people dance to and like Using other lyrics and melodies as a launch to write new songs			Knowing where other members of band are going in the song when playing live	Ability to determine what songs will work in the market
	Making mistakes when playing leads to new base lines or chord structures Playing with different musicians to develop alternative styles of playing	Able to call upon a range of styles from early days in social clubs			Ability to play different styles
	Using deep emotions and experience to write songs Building relationships with agent and gig managers Building relationships with other musicians Constant need to ensure that music is prioritized with other important things in life			Trust-based relationship when recording	Relationship with audience Reputation to satisfy audience

Author	Discover	Delay	Dispose	Diffuse	Deliver
Explicit					
	Research studies New books Newspapers Specialist journals and magazines Web sites Conferences Feedback from training course Random walks Colleagues' ideas Feedback from readers Ideas from Sara Rowe Strap lines from Paul Oliver	Memory of ideas Word files Psion log Work experiences Life experiences Workbook	Forced reading of new topics Challenge from Dave Chitty Meet new people and grow network Presenting ideas at conference Running pilot courses Testing with colleagues	Conferences Team colleagues Articles and white papers Net conversation Social meetings Training sessions Random e-mails with other strangers Meeting with FT design team	Book Articles Net publications Journal papers Short courses
	Software packages Randomization with Carmel McDonald	Software capability			Presentation skills to sell ideas PC skills Web skills
	Feedback from readers	Challenging goals and dates Relationship with editor Carmel's passion	Relationship with previous editor	Colleagues to share beliefs	Conferences and seminars to market ideas Relationship management with editor Relationship management with journal managers

Author	Discover	Delay	Dispose	Diffuse	Deliver
Tactic					
	New trends Intuitive discovery and creation of ideas	Personal stories and metaphors Feeling for what will work Shifting trends in the market	Work with peers	Beliefs with peer group	Intuitive ideas at training courses
	Web walks Client ideas				
	What people want to read about Feedback from training course	Feel for what people want to read		Motivation from Carmel and Dave Support from colleagues	Open and honest views Desire for feedback

Bibliography

Preface

1 Harford, B, *Greenham Common: Women at the Wire*, ed Sarah Hopkins.

Chapter 1

1 Drucker, P, *Post-Capitalist Society*, Butterworth-Heinemann, Oxford, 1993.
2 Handy, C, *The New Alchemist*, Hutchinson, 1999.

Chapter 2

1 Schultz, T, *Investing in People, The Economics of Population Quality*, Berkeley and Los Angeles, CA, University of California, 1981.
2 Stewart, T A, *Intellectual Capital*, Nicholas Brealey, 1997.
3 Stewart, T A, *Intellectual Capital*, Nicholas Brealey Publishing, 1997.
4 Snowden, D, *A Framework for Creating a Sustainable Programme, from Knowledge Management – a Real Guide*, CBI, Caspian Publishing, 1994.
5 Haak, T, and Lekanne Deprez, F (KPMG The Netherlands) 2nd World Business Dialogue on Rethinking Knowledge, Cologne, Germany, 3–4 March 1999.
6 Drucker, P, *Post-Capitalist Society*, Butterworth-Heinemann, Oxford, 1993.
7 Drucker, P, *Post-Capitalist Society*, Butterworth-Heinemann, Oxford, 1993.
8 Haak, T, and Lekanne Deprez, F (KPMG The Netherlands) 2nd World Business Dialogue on Rethinking Knowledge, Cologne, Germany, 3–4 March 1999.
9 Andriessen, D, http://kpmg.interact.nl/
10 Senge, P, *The Fifth Discipline*, Century Business, 1990.
11 Scott, M, *Time Management*, Century Business, 1992.
12 Cooke, S, and Slack, N, *Making Management Decisions*, Prentice Hall International, London, 1991.
13 Mack, R P, *Planning on Uncertainty – Decision Making in business and government administration*, Wiley – Interscience, 1971.
14 March, J, and Simon, H, *Organizations*, Wiley, 1958.
15 Leonard-Bartin, D, *Wellsprings of Knowledge*, Harvard Business School Press, 1995.

Chapter 3

1 Seely Brown, J, and Gray, E S, *The People Are the Company*, http://www.fastcompany.com/online/01/people.html, November 1995 *Fast Company*, Premiere, p 78.
2 Egan, *Working the Shadow Side*, Jossey-Bass, 1994.
3 Janis, I, *Victims of Groupthink*, Boston, Houghton Mifflin, 1972, rev. 1983.
4 Goleman, D, *Vital Lies, Simple Truths*, Bloomsbury, London, 1997.
5 Grove, A, *Only the Paranoid Survive*, Currency Book by Doubleday, New York, 1998.

Chapter 5

1 Nonaka, I, and Takeuchi, T, *The Knowledge Creating Company*, Oxford University Press, 1995.
2 Sanchez, R, 'Managing Articulate Knowledge in Competence-based Competition', in *Strategic Learning and Management*, Wiley, 1997.
3 Smith, G, *Knowledge Management*, February 2000, 3 (5), 27.
4 Sanchez, R, *Strategic Learning and Knowledge Management*, Wiley, 1997.
5 Dixon, N, *The Organizational Learning Cycle*, McGraw-Hill, 1994.
6 Chun Wei Choo, *The Knowing Organization*, Oxford University Press, New York, 1998.
7 Dryden, G, and Vos, J, *The Learning Revolution, Accelerated Learning Systems*, Aston, 1994.
8 *The Penguin Dictionary of Psychology*, 1985.
9 Goldman, D, *Emotional Intelligence*, Bloomsbury, London, 1996.
10 Edvinsson, L, and Malone, M, *Intellectual Capital*, Piatkus, London, 1998.
11 Stewart, T, *Intellectual Capital*, Nicholas Brealey, 1997.
12 Peters, T, *The Brand You 50*, Alfred A. Knopf, Inc., 1999.
13 Machlup, F, 'Knowledge and Knowledge Production', *Knowledge: Its creation, distribution and economic significance*), 1, Princeton, NJ, Princeton University Press, 1980.

Chapter 6

1 Barclay, O, and Murray, P C, http://www.knowledge-at-work.com/whatis.htm
2 http://www.cio.com/archive/021598_excerpt. html
3 Huy, Nguyen, 'Emotional Capability and Corporate Change', *FT Mastering Strategy*, 13 December 1999.
4 Cooper and Sawaf, *Executive EQ*, Orion Business, 1997.
5 Cooper and Sawaf, *Executive EQ*, Orion Business, 1997.
6 *Great Scientific Discoveries*, Chambers, 1991.
7 Rubin, H, http://www.fastcompany.com/online/29/paranoia.html, *Fast Company*, 29, 330, November 1999.
8 Roberts, P, 'Group Genius,' *Fast Company* 11, 202, October 1997, http://www.fastcompany.com/online/11/genius.htm/

Chapter 7

1 James, W, *Cognitive Psychology*, Hodder & Stoughton, London, 1997.

2 Gross, R, and McIlveen, R, *Cognitive Psychology*, Hodder & Stoughton, 1997.

3 LeDoux, J, *The Emotional Brain*, Weidenfield & Nicolson, London, 1998.

4 Gleitman, H, *Basic Psychology*, W W Norton & Company, New York, 1999.

5 Kurzweil, R, *The Age of Spiritual Machines*, Phoenix, Orion Books, London, 1999.

6 Huy, Nguyen, 'Emotional Capability and Corporate Change,' *FT Mastering Strategy*, 13 December 1999.

7 Kim, Daniel, 'The Link Between Individual and Organizational Learning,' *Sloan Management Review*, 1993.

8 Moorman, C, and Miner, A, 'Organizational Improvization and Organizational Memory,' *Academy of Management Review*, 1998, 23 (4), 698–723.

9 Nelson, R, and Winter, S, *An Evolutionary Theory of Economic Change*, Harvard University Press, 1982.

10 Nahapiet, J, and Ghoshal, S, 'Social Capital, Intellectual Capital and the Organizational Advantage,' *Academy of Management Review*, 1998, 23 (2), 242–256.

11 Coleman, J, 'Social Capital in the Creation of Human Capital,' *American Journal of Sociology 94*, 1988, S995–S120.

12 Fukuyama Financial Trust, *The Social Virtues and the Creation of Prosperity*, Hamilton, London, 1995.

13 Nahapiet, J, and Ghoshal, S, 'Social Capital, Intellectual Capital and the Organizational Advantage,' *Academy of Management Review*, 1998, 23 (2), 242–256.

14 Burt, R, 'The Contingent Value of Social Capital,' *Administrative Science Quarterly*, June 1997, 339–365.

15 Burt, R, 'The Contingent Value of Social Capital,' *Administrative Science Quarterly*, June 1997, 339–365.

16 Kogut, B, and Zander, U, 'What do Firms do? Co-ordination, Identity and Learning,' 1996, *Organization Science,* 7: 502–518.

Chapter 8

1 *Sunday Times* appointment page, advert by GE Capital GCF Europe, 31 October 1999.

2 Hite, S, *Sex and Business*, Pearson Education, London, 1999.

3 Battram, A, http://world.std.com/~lo/96.09/0589.html, 10 December 1999.

4 Schein, E H, 'How can Organizations Learn Faster? The Challenge of Entering the Green Room,' *Sloan Management Review*, Winter 1993, 87.

5 Nicolini, M, 'The Social Construction of Organizational Learning: Conceptual and Practical Issues in the Field,' *Human Relations*, 48 (7), 1995.

6 DiBella, T, Nevis and Gould, 'Understanding Organizational Learning Capability, *Journal of Management Studies*, May, 1996.

7 Carnal, C, *Managing Change in Organizations*, Prentice Hall, London, 1995.
8 Starbuck, W H, 'Unlearning Learning Ineffective or Obsolete Technologies,' *International Journal of Technology Management*, 11: 725–737, 1996.
9 Kanter, R, *The Change Masters*, Unwin, 1984.

Chapter 9

1 McMaster, M, http://www.co-i-l.com/coil/knowledge-garden/cop/mmintro.shtml, 12 December 1999.
2 Spaeth, E, and Hamilton, P, *What a Lawyer Needs to Learn, from Tacit Knowledge in Professional Practice*, edited by Sternberg, R, and Horvath, J, Lawrence Erlbaum Associates, Mahwah, New Jersey, 1999.
3 Schein, E, *Organizational Psychology*, Prentice Hall, 1988.
4 Wolfe, T, *The Bonfire of the Vanities*, Picador, 1987.
5 Stewart and Jones, *TA Today*, Lifespace Publishing, 1987.
6 Seely Brown, J, and Gray, E S, *The People Are the Company*, http://www.fastcompany.com/online/01/people.html, November 1995: *Fast Company*, Premiere, p 78.

Chapter 10

1 Webber, A, *Are You a Star at Work?*, http://www.fastcompany.com/online/15/star.html, 5 January 2000.
2 Matson, E, *How to Get a Piece of the Action*, http://www.fastcompany.com/online/05/action.html, 5 January 2000.
3 Webber, A M, *Are You a Star at Work?*, http://www.fastcompany.com/online/15/star.html, 5 January 2000.
4 Webber, A M, *Are You a Star at Work?*, http://www.fastcompany.com/online/15/star.html, 5 January 2000.
5 Webber, A M, *How to Get Them to Show You the Money*, http://www.fastcompany.com/online/19/showmoney.html, 5 January 2000.

Chapter 12

1 Encyclopedia Britannica, http://search.eb.com/bol/topic?idxref=153814, 31 December 1999.
2 Encyclopedia Britannica, http://search.eb.com/cgi-bin/dictionary?va=amateur
3 David Blunkett, Secretary of State for Education and Employment, http://www.lifelonglearning.co.uk/greenpaper/index.htm
4 Rogers, E, *Diffusion of Innovations*, 4th edn, The Free Press, 1995.
5 'Lincoln, Abraham' *Encyclopedia Britannica Online*. http://search.eb.com/bol/topic?eu=114491&sctn=11
6 Patel, V, Arocha, J, and Kaufman, D, 'Expertise and Tacit Knowledge in Medicine,' in *Tacit Knowledge in Professional Practice*, edited by Sternberg, R, and Horvath, J, Lawrence Erlbaum Associates, New Jersey.
7 Davis, R, http://wkweb5.cableinet.co.uk/elsham/gt_esc

Chapter 13

1 Peters, T, 'Brand You,' http://www.fastcompany.com/brandyou/future.html, *Fast Company Magazine*, August/September 1997.
2 *Forbes Magazine*, http://www.forbes.com/Forbes/99/0322/6306188a.html, 2 January 1999.
3 Schwartz, P, *The Art of the Long View*, Currency Doubleday, New York, 1991.
4 Mazzie, M, http://www.cio.com/archive/enterprise/101599_ic.html

Chapter 14

1 Egan, *Working the Shadow Side*, Jossey-Bass, 1994.
2 Luft, J, and Ingham, H, *The Johari Window: A Graphic Model for Interpersonal Relations*, University of California, Western Training Laboratory, 1955.

Index